GAY & LESBIAN STATS

A Pocket Guide of Facts and Figures

Edited by
Bennett L. Singer and David Deschamps

with an introduction by Congressman Gerry E. Studds
and a preface by Dr. Stephanie Sanders, Director, Kinsey Institute

D1369894

THE NEW PRESS
New York

Published in the United States by The New Press, New York
Distributed by W. W. Norton & Company, Inc.
500 Fifth Avenue, New York, NY 10110

LIBRARY OF CONGRESS CATALOGING-IN-PUBLICATION DATA

Singer, Bennett L.
    Gay & lesbian stats : a pocket guide of facts and
figures / Bennett L. Singer and David Deschamps.
        p. cm.
    Includes bibliographical references.
    ISBN 1-56584-155-7
    1. Gay men—United States—Statistics. 2. Lesbians—
United States—Statistics. I. Deschamps, David. II. Title.
III. Title: Gay and lesbian stats.
HQ76.3.U5S59 1994
305.9′0664′021—dc20   94-4123

First Edition

Book design by Laura Lindgren

Established in 1990 as a major alternative to the large, commercial publishing houses, The New Press is the first full-scale nonprofit American book publisher outside of the university presses. The Press is operated editorially in the public interest, rather than for private gain; it is committed to publishing in innovative ways works of educational, cultural, and community value that, despite their intellectual merits, might not normally be "commercially" viable. The New Press's editorial offices are located at The City University of New York.

Printed in the United States of America

94 95 96 97   10 9 8 7 6 5 4 3 2 1

(ONTENT)

NOTE FROM THE EDITORS

This book presents a series of snapshots of lesbians and gay men. Culled from hundreds of sources, these snapshots go a long way toward revealing where the gay and lesbian community stands twenty-five years after the Stonewall uprising of 1969. Our goal was not to compile an all-inclusive reference work; rather, we set out to create an album of statistics that illuminate the triumphs and challenges facing lesbians and gay men in their varied roles as citizens and as soldiers, as parents and as children, in politics and in the arts, at work and at play.

We have made every effort to include only the most up-to-date information and to represent the full breadth of the lesbian and gay community. In virtually every area, however, we have found that the statistics available on lesbian and gay issues reflect an unmistakable bias toward college-educated white males. We genuinely hope that this collection will inspire research that reflects a broader spectrum of lesbian, gay, and bisexual lives and voices.

This book would not have been possible without the participation of dozens of groups and organizations that serve the lesbian, gay, and bisexual community. We are greatly indebted to these groups for their vigilance in collecting data and for their willingness to share their research files with us. For their helpful comments on the manuscript, we are grateful to Jamie Penney of the Boston Women's Health Book Collective, Wayne Dynes, Gordon Thomas, and Paul Singer. Research assistance for the project was provided by Antoinette Eng, Alexandra Gerber, and Julia Sullivan; in addition, the book benefited from the research expertise of librarians at the New York Public Library, the San Francisco Public Library, and the Boston Public Library.

Special thanks go to Roz Parr of A Different Light Bookstore, Rachel Singer Sullivan, Kate Dyer, Mark Agrast, Margaret Harter, Jack Garrity, Robyn Hutt, Susie Bright, and Margo for their support and assistance.

And, finally, we would like to express our gratitude to our friend and editor, Diane Wachtell, and to André Schiffrin, Akiko Takano, Max Gordon, Ellen Reeves, and the entire staff of The New Press for their backing of this project and their ongoing commitment to publishing innovative material on lesbian and gay issues.

Bennett L. Singer and David Deschamps

INTRODUCTION

Some forty years ago, a popular volume was published called *How to Lie with Statistics.* As its author put it, "A well-wrapped statistic is better than Hitler's 'big lie'; it misleads, yet it cannot be pinned on you."

As lesbians and gay men, we have all too often found ourselves at the mercy of such well-wrapped statistics. Yet we do not have at our disposal a solid base of information with which to refute the big lies of our own time.

We are perhaps in greater need of sound, factual information about ourselves than any group of people in our society. Like every community, ours has ancestors, and we want to know as much as we can about them. But because our consciousness of ourselves as a community is so very new, we must reconstruct our history out of shards and fragments culled from the few records of our past that were kept or deemed worthy of transmission to us.

It is also important to us to document the truth because we have paid such a heavy price for dishonesty—not only the lies of those who wish us ill, but also the fear that still compels so many of our sisters and brothers to lead lives of deception and concealment.

The reality of that fear made it extraordinarily difficult to assemble the information contained in this book. How do you measure a community that is still largely invisible? In 1989, I released a report by the Defense Personnel Security Research and Education Center (PERSEREC) which concluded that "having a same-gender or an opposite-gender orientation is unrelated to job performance in the same way as is being left- or right-handed." Yet, as the authors of this volume note, only when the truth of that statement is universally acknowledged will it be possible to get an accurate count.

No one, for example, can tell you the number of lesbians and gay men serving in the Congress of the United States. The only "facts" we can categorically assert are that after I made my public declaration on the floor of the House of Representatives in 1983 there was one openly gay member; since then the number has doubled. I fervently hope that by the time the second edition of this book appears, the membership of the smallest congressional caucus will have multiplied again.

And we will need that second edition because the statistics are continually changing as our community itself evolves. Thus, the editors inform us, in 1969 there were 50 lesbian and gay organizations in the

United States; today there are more than 2500. Among the other remarkable statistics you will read here is the fact that there are today between one and five million lesbian mothers and between one and three million gay fathers in the United States, raising from six to fourteen million children. And if a few short years ago no jurisdiction protected lesbians and gay men from discrimination in the workplace, today we find 8 states, 130 municipalities and more than 100 major corporations that have enacted such protections.

Not every fact about gay people (or any other group) is a cause for pride. But I believe that when all of the facts are put together, the picture that emerges will be a human one. And that is cause for immense pride.

We must no longer allow ourselves to be victimized by distortions and half-truths. Neither must we be content to perpetuate falsehoods that seem to serve our purposes. We have all played the numbers game, as though it really matters whether we represent 10 percent or 4 percent of the population. We must learn to cherish the whole truth so we can learn to embrace ourselves, warts and all.

If this book helps us in that process, it will have performed an invaluable public service.

Gerry E. Studds
Washington, D.C.

PREFACE

Statistics can inform or mislead. The difference between these outcomes rests on understanding the numbers themselves—what are they saying, about what group, and for what time period—and on awareness of methods used for data collection. The way in which questions are worded, the training of researchers collecting data, and the use of interviews versus written questionnaires can all have a profound influence on findings from studies, particularly when dealing with sensitive topics related to human sexuality. It is important to consider these key issues when trying to reconcile survey results that seem highly discrepant.

Most sex research has used "nonprobability" sampling procedures, in which specific groups such as college students or gay organizations are asked to participate in a study. The degree to which these findings may tell us about college students or gay people in general depends on the degree to which the sample reflects the target population as a whole. The questions to ask are, "How similar were the people studied to the group in general?" and, "Were people recruited to participate in the study in ways that would bias the sample?"

The demand for information on sexual behaviors related to AIDS has led to an increase in studies utilizing "probability" samples, in which all members of the population have an equal chance of being selected. But if we do not know the percentage of people who belong to a certain minority group—such as the percentage of gays and lesbians in the population—we must rely on the assumption that they are randomly distributed in the population and that the number in the study will be proportional to the number in the general population. There is some question about the validity of this assumption: certainly there are gay districts in which the proportion of persons who are homosexual is substantially higher than it is just a few blocks away.

Regardless of the sampling technique, most sexual behavior surveys have 60 to 70 percent response rates. That means that the sexual behavior of 30 to 40 percent of prospective respondents is unknown. With sanctions against same-sex activity in 20 states and widespread discrimination against homosexuals, many gay men and lesbians may fear that revealing their homosexuality to researchers would cause problems socially and professionally.

Perhaps the greatest difficulty in comparing findings derives from differences in how homosexuality is defined. A person who has had a same-sex sexual interaction may or may not consider himself or herself to be homosexual—and whether that person *calls* himself or herself homosexual on a survey is another question altogether. Furthermore, the time period encompassed by the question can greatly influence findings. For example, a person may not have had a same-sex partner during the past year but may have had one or several during his or her lifetime.

Media coverage often distorts the findings of studies that have examined the percentage of gays in the general population. Much attention has focused on comparison of lower figures from some recent probability studies to the widely used but often misrepresented 10 percent figure of Kinsey. Although the Kinsey data were not obtained using probability sampling techniques, there were certain strengths of the research that the more recent studies lack. The Kinsey data were obtained in interviews conducted by highly trained professionals; this method afforded an opportunity to build rapport and ask clarifying questions when inconsistencies were noted. In 1979, the authors of *The Kinsey Data* recalculated figures from the basic sample, eliminating prisoners and volunteers from groups with known sexual bias, such as gay organizations. This recalculation revealed that 9.9 percent of college-educated white males and 12.7 percent of those with less than a college education had 21 or more partners of the same sex and/or 51 or more homosexual experiences. Considering the differences in methodologies, Dr. Paul Gebhard, coauthor of *The Kinsey Data,* concluded in a recent article that the Kinsey figure of 10 percent is not a bad estimate of reality. Clearly, more research is needed on how different methodological approaches influence such estimates. Only with this knowledge, combined with estimates from studies using diverse approaches, will we gain a clearer picture of how many homosexuals are in the general population.

Readers of this book may ask: Why is there so much recent interest in the question of what proportion of the population is homosexual? Could it be that the difference between 10 percent and 1 percent would justify differential treatment legally and socially? Should civil rights protections be based on such numbers? If so, whose numbers and what cutoff will be used? How much power will be given to statistics?

Stephanie A. Sanders, Ph.D.
Interim Director, The Kinsey Institute for Research
in Sex, Gender, and Reproduction
Indiana University

"A STATISTICAL BATTLEGROUND":

COUNTING LESBIANS AND GAY MEN IN THE UNITED STATES

"Homosexuals as a group are the first, second, or third most numerous minority in the U.S.—depending on which variation of the estimate is used."

John C. Gonsiorek and James D. Weinrich,
Homosexuality: Research Implications for Public Policy, 1991

Although dozens of studies have been conducted to determine how many gay men and lesbians reside in the United States, definitive numbers continue to elude researchers for two reasons. First is the difficulty in defining "homosexual": Does a person have to engage in same-sex sexual activity to be counted as gay or lesbian? Or is it a matter of how one defines oneself, regardless of behavior? Can a celibate priest be gay? Would an army sergeant who identifies herself as a lesbian but engages in no lesbian acts while in the armed forces be considered a homosexual in the eyes of researchers studying sexual conduct in the military?

The stigma attached to being lesbian or gay accounts for the second major difficulty in ascertaining accurate population figures in the United States. Gross underreporting in many studies, especially those that involve face-to-face interviews with researchers, is pervasive. Until stating that one is gay or lesbian is as noncontroversial as stating that one is right-handed or left-handed, it will be impossible to get an accurate count of the number of homosexual and bisexual people in the United States.

The table below contains results of nearly twenty studies that have investigated the prevalence of homosexuality since Alfred Kinsey's landmark study published in 1948. But as the table indicates, comparing different surveys' results is not easy, since some document the number of same-sex experiences while others document the number of people who identify themselves as gay or lesbian. Note, too, that these surveys were conducted with a wide variety of methods, ranging from anonymous, random samples to a self-selected group of *Playboy* readers.

STUDY (YEAR)	PERCENTAGE OF SAMPLE THAT IS GAY OR LESBIAN	COMMENTS
Kinsey et al. (1948)	10% of males reported being more or less exclusively homosexual for at least three years between ages 16 and 55; 37% of all males had some homosexual contact to orgasm	Pioneering study of 5,300 white men; criticized for using non-probability sample that included prisoners and college students. These sampling flaws were addressed in 1979 reanalysis by Gebhard et al. that yielded almost identical results of 9.9% and 34%, respectively.
Kinsey et al. (1953)	2%–6% of females reported being more or less exclusively homosexual between ages 20 and 35; 13% of females had some homosexual contact to orgasm	Study of 5,940 white females
Psychology Today (1970)	37% of male and 12% of female readers had some homosexual contact to orgasm	Self-selected sampling of 20,000 readers
Gagnon and Simon (1973)	5%–6% of males and 3% of females had substantial homosexual experiences; 30% of males had some homosexual contact to orgasm	Reanalysis of Kinsey data focusing on the college population
Hunt (1974)	7% of males and 3% of females had homosexual experiences during more than three years; 25% of males had some homosexual contact to orgasm	Questionnaire survey of 2,036 people; not a representative sample

STUDY (YEAR)	PERCENTAGE OF SAMPLE THAT IS GAY OR LESBIAN	COMMENTS
Smith and Garner (1976)	40% of male athletes had sex to the point of orgasm with another man at least twice within the prior two years	Small sample (82) of members of the National College Athletic Association, with large margin of error
Pietropinto and Simenauer (1977)	3.1% of males said they engage in sex with men and women	Large-scale (nonrandom) survey of 4,066 men; self-administered written questionnaire
Playboy (1983)	35% of men and 22% of women reported some homosexual contact to orgasm during adolescence; 10% of men and 12% of women reported homosexual experience since adolescence	Self-selected sampling of 100,000 male and female readers
Cameron (1985)	5.8% of males identified themselves as gay; 3.1% of females identified themselves as lesbian	Questions have been raised about bias in the survey; researcher also mis-quoted his own findings in national publication
Hatfield (1989)	6.2% of men and women identified themselves as homosexual	Telephone survey by the San Francisco Examiner
Fay et al. (1989)	20.3% of adult males had some homosexual contact to orgasm	Comparison from national sample surveys from 1970 and 1988
Harry (1990)	3.7% of males identified themselves as gay or bisexual	National telephone survey included one question on same-sex attraction; sample of 663 males
Sell et al. (1990)	Males who report same-sex behavior since age 15: 11.6% (U.S.); 7.8% (U.K.); 11.6% (France)	Random survey of large number of men (5,700); used well-trained field staff to personally interview subjects

STUDY (YEAR)	PERCENTAGE OF SAMPLE THAT IS GAY OR LESBIAN	COMMENTS
Rogers and Turner (1991)	5%–7% of males experienced some same-sex contact as adults	Results of five probability samples from 1970–1990
Smith (1991)	5%–6% had some homosexual contact to orgasm since age 18; less than 1% of sample exclusively gay	Taken from National Opinion Research Center's General Social Surveys; criticized for not using professional sex researchers and lack of extensive interviews
NORC (1989–1993)	2.8% of males identified themselves as gay; 2.5% of females identified themselves as lesbian	Same as above
Johnson and Spira (1992)	Subjects that had homosexual experience in last five years: Britain: 6.1% of males; France: 4.1% of males and 2.6% of females	Large representative samples: 18,000 in Britain and 20,000 in France
Janus and Janus (1993)	9% of males and 5% of females reported "ongoing" or "frequent" homosexual experiences; 4% of males and 2% of females self-identified as homosexual	Cross-sectional nationwide survey of 2,765 men and women who answered questionnaire; supplemented by some interviews
Billy (1993)	2% of sexually active males reported same-sex experience in last ten years; 1% of males identified themselves as exclusively homosexual during the same time period	Batelle Human Affairs Research Center study of HIV risk in the sexual behavior of men ages 20–39; criticized for lack of professional sex researchers and lack of extensive interviews

"Gay people have taken on many of the traits of ethnicity to assert their political will. Increasingly organized through an indigenous press, in neighborhoods, at work, and at church, lesbians and gay men have forged a social movement that—like all others—seeks to give them a voice in their own future and to defend themselves against the violence of the state and of others."

Barry Adam, *The Rise of a Gay and Lesbian Movement*, 1987

The surge in lesbian and gay activism over the past twenty-five years is clearly documented in statistics that chart the number of social and political organizations that have sprung up in lesbian and gay communities across the country. Similarly, the growing ranks of "out" elected officials reflect the strides that gay men and lesbians have made in securing a voice within the legislative arena.

ACTIVISM

The first homosexual rights group, the Scientific Humanitarian Committee, was founded in Berlin by Magnus Hirschfeld on May 15, 1897. [1]

The first formally organized lesbian or gay movement group in the United States, the Society for Human Rights, was chartered by the City of Chicago in 1924. The group's stated mission was to "promote and protect the interests of people who by reasons of mental and physical abnormalities are abused and hindered in the legal pursuit of happiness." [1]

The Mattachine Society, founded in 1951 in Los Angeles, and Daughters of Bilitis, founded in 1955 in San Francisco, were the first post–World War II civil rights organizations for gay men and lesbians, respectively. [1]

In 1969, there were 50 lesbian and gay organizations in the United States. [2]

In 1973, there were 800 lesbian and gay organizations in the United States. [2]

According to *The Gayellow Pages*, there are currently at least 2,500 lesbian and gay social, political, religious, student, and cultural organizations in the United States. [3]

Founded in 1973, the National Gay and Lesbian Task Force is the oldest national lesbian and gay civil rights advocacy group. It has 32,000 members, 23 full-time staff members, and a $3.3 million budget for 1993. [2]

Founded in 1980, the Human Rights Campaign Fund (HRCF) is the nation's largest national gay and lesbian political organization, with some 80,000 members, 38 staff members, and an operating budget of $6 million for 1993. [4]

In 1992, HRCF contributed $785,000 to congressional candidates through its political action committee. Of the more than 4,000 federal political action committees, HRCF's is the 42nd largest. [4]

The Log Cabin Federation, a lesbian and gay Republican group, has 5,000 members in 25 chapters nationwide. The National Log Cabin Political Action Committee contributed $60,000 to Republican candidates in 1992. [5, 6]

Founded in New York City in 1987 by the gay playwright Larry Kramer and other activists, ACT UP, the AIDS Coalition To Unleash Power, is credited with accelerating the drug approval process, lowering the cost of drugs that treat AIDS, and forcing presidential candidates to address AIDS. Worldwide, ACT UP had 79 chapters as of November 1993. [7, 8]

Founded in 1966, the National Organization for Women (NOW) introduced its first resolution on lesbian rights in 1971. In 1991, Patricia Ireland became the first NOW president to say publicly that she has a woman lover. [9]

The first American gay rights demonstration took place at the Whitehall Induction Center in New York City on September 19,1963, protesting discrimination by the military. [10]

On the night of June 27–28, 1969, New York City police raided the Stonewall Inn in Greenwich Village. It was the sixth raid of a gay bar in New York City within three weeks. Police were surprised when drag queens, lesbians, street people, and bar patrons fought back, hurling jeers and later stones and parking meters at the officers. This demonstration of collective resistance, known as the Stonewall Rebellion, was a watershed in the modern movement for lesbian and gay rights and liberation. [1]

The first gay and lesbian pride march took place in New York City on June 28, 1970, commemorating the Stonewall uprising of the year before. More than 2,000 people participated. [1, 10]

Washington, D.C., held its first Black Lesbian and Gay Pride celebration in 1991, attracting "hundreds of participants." [11]

At least 44 cities worldwide held gay and lesbian pride celebrations in 1993. New York City's celebration attracted an estimated 750,000 participants and spectators. [12]

The Los Angeles Gay and Lesbian Community Services Center, founded in 1971, is the largest of the nation's at least 50 lesbian and gay community centers. [13, 14]

In 1988, people of color made up 17% of the Los Angeles Gay and Lesbian Community Services Center's staff. In 1992, people of color made up 40% of the staff and 25% of the managers. Women represented 50% of the staff and managers. [13]

Lesbians, gay men, bisexuals, and their supporters have held three Marches on Washington to demand equal rights and liberation. Attendance figures have been highly contested:

	U.S. Park Service Police	*Time* Magazine	*The Advocate*
October 14, 1979	25,000–50,000	Not reported	100,000
October 11, 1987	200,000	Not reported	Reported both Park Service Police estimate and organizers' count: 650,000
April 25, 1993	300,000	Reported both Park Service Police count and organizers' estimate cited as 1 million	Reported both Park Service Police count and organizers' estimate cited as 1.1 million

ELECTED OFFICIALS

The first openly gay or lesbian elected official was Kathy Kozachenko, who was chosen for the Ann Arbor, Michigan, city council in 1974. [10]

The nation's first African American lesbian elected official was Sherry Harris, who was elected to the city council of Seattle, Washington, in 1991. [10]

In 1980, there were 5 openly gay or lesbian elected officials in the United States. [15]

In January 1994 there were 133 openly gay or lesbian elected officials in federal, state, and municipal offices, including Congressmen Barney Frank and Gerry Studds (both of Massachusetts). This figure represents .03% of the 450,000 elected officials in the United States. [16]

NATIONAL POLITICS

The Democratic Party first adopted a platform plank favoring lesbian and gay rights in 1980. [10]

13 pro-gay speakers addressed the 1992 Democratic National Convention in New York, which was attended by 108 openly gay or lesbian delegates, alternates, and party officials. [18]

No Republican Party platform has endorsed gay or lesbian rights. To the contrary, the 1992 Republican Party platform stated that "we oppose efforts by the Democratic Party to include sexual preference as a protected minority receiving preferential status under civil rights statutes at the federal, state and local level." [19]

In the 1992 presidential election, an estimated 93.6% of the lesbian and gay community voted, representing 17 million persons (based on Kinsey's estimates). [20]

Bill Clinton received 89.2% of the lesbian and gay vote in 1992. [20]

A *Newsweek* poll of 460 lesbians and gay men in May 1993 found that
- 88% approved of Bill Clinton's job as president
- 91% thought Clinton "cares about people like me"
- 74% thought Clinton was keeping his campaign promises

- 62% thought gaining equal rights in terms of jobs and the legal system was the most important priority for the lesbian and gay movement
- 23% thought "winning acceptance for the gay lifestyle" was the most important priority for the lesbian and gay movement. [21]

As of the fall of 1993, Bill Clinton had appointed 25 openly gay men and lesbians to positions within his administration. Among them was Roberta Achtenberg, who became the highest-ranking "out" gay or lesbian in the executive branch of the federal government when she was appointed assistant secretary of fair housing and equal opportunity in the Department of Housing and Urban Development. [17, 22]

As of the fall of 1993, no president had ever appointed an openly gay or lesbian person to any of the 1,000 federal judgeships. [23]

SOURCES

1. Barry D. Adam, *The Rise of a Gay and Lesbian Movement,* Boston: Twayne, 1987.
2. National Gay and Lesbian Task Force, Washington, D.C., 1993.
3. *Gayellow Pages,* New York: Renaissance House, 1993.
4. Human Rights Campaign Fund, Washington, D.C., 1993.
5. "Homosexuals and Politics: To the Tolerant the Money," *The Economist,* October 3, 1992.
6. Daniel Willson, "Back To Bush?" *The Advocate,* August 13, 1992.
7. Sally Chew, "What's Going Down with ACT UP," *OUT,* November 1993.
8. Jeffrey Schmalz, "Whatever Happened To AIDS?" *New York Times Magazine,* November 28, 1993.
9. Donna Minkowitz, "Patricia Ireland Takes the Reins," *The Advocate,* December 17, 1991.
10. Lynne Yamaguchi Fletcher, *The First Gay Pope and Other Records,* Boston: Alyson, 1992.
11. "Dossier," *The Advocate,* July 2, 1991.
12. Heritage of Pride, Inc., New York, 1993.
13. John Gallagher, "Torie Osborn: 'We Have a Righteous Skepticism,' " *The Advocate,* August 13, 1992.
14. The New York Gay and Lesbian Community Services Center, 1993.
15. "Out and About," *The Economist,* July 27, 1991.
16. Jane Gross, "Gay Candidate Making History in a State Race," *New York Times,* January 4, 1994.
17. The Victory Fund, Washington, D.C., 1993.
18. Bill Turque, "Gays Under Fire," *Newsweek,* September 14, 1992.
19. Republican Party platform, quoted in *1992 Congressional Quarterly Almanac.*
20. Overlooked Opinions, Inc., Chicago, 1993.
21. Howard Fineman, "Marching to the Mainstream," *Newsweek,* May 3, 1993.
22. "Achtung, Roberta baby!" *The Advocate,* June 29, 1993.
23. Stephen Reinhardt, "Why Should Federal Judges Have To Hide in the Closet?" *Washington Post,* October 31, 1993.

The Harvard AIDS Institute estimates that there will be 100 million HIV infections worldwide by the year 2000.

As activists have long pointed out, AIDS is clearly *not* a gay disease; world statistics demonstrate that the way the epidemic has unfolded in the United States is not representative of international trends. Nevertheless, in the United States, AIDS has had a profound effect on the gay and lesbian community. Many aspects of the impact of the disease have been well documented, but one phenomenon has proved difficult to measure— the way that the disease has reshaped alliances and forged new coalitions within and outside gay and lesbian communities.

46% of the American public surveyed in 1988 said they have "a lot" of sympathy for people with AIDS. 17% said they have "a lot" of sympathy for people with AIDS who contracted the disease through homosexual contact. [1]

1 in 10 respondents to a 1988 Gallup Poll reported avoiding, or planning to avoid, homosexuals in order to remain uninfected with the AIDS virus. [1]

In 1990, 1 in 4 participants in a national survey thought it was "very likely" or "somewhat likely" that someone would contract AIDS from eating at a restaurant where the cook has the AIDS virus; 19% thought they could catch AIDS from public toilets. [2]

WORLD STATS

13 million people worldwide are infected with HIV, the virus that causes AIDS. Someone in the world is infected with HIV every 15 to 20 seconds. [3, 4, 5]

According to the World Health Organization, 75% of the people infected with HIV worldwide were infected through heterosexual sex. [5]

More than 2.5 million people, including a half-million children, have died of AIDS worldwide. [3, 5]

The best projection of the total number of world AIDS deaths by the year 1995 is 4,693,500. This estimate breaks down as follows:
- 67.8% in Sub-Saharan Africa
- 8.6% in Latin America
- 10.1% in North America
- 5.1% in Western Europe

- 4.9% in Southeast Asia
- 2.6% in the Caribbean
- .3% in Northeast Asia
- .2% in Oceania
- .2% in Eastern Europe
- .2% in Southeastern Mediterranean [6]

As of 1991, 29 countries had imposed some restrictions based on HIV status, while 15 countries routinely checked gay men for HIV without their consent. [6]

Cuba is the only country that mandates automatic hospitalization of all people infected with HIV. [6]

U.S. STATS

An estimated 1.5 million Americans—1 of every 100 men and 1 of every 600 women—are infected with HIV. [7]

As of October 1993, 339,250 AIDS cases had been reported in the United States. [8]

Nearly 50% of Americans with AIDS are people of color. [5]

The rate of HIV infection among American adolescents is doubling each year. [9]

As of August 1992, 1 in 5 people with AIDS were in their twenties and probably became infected in their teens. [10]

In a comparison of the source of exposure to HIV in North, South, and Latin Americans between 1987 and 1990, the rate of transmission by homosexual contact dropped in every geographical area. [6]

Between 1987 and 1990, the percentage of HIV infections transmitted by heterosexual contact and drug use increased in every geographical area, by up to 37% and 22%, respectively. [6]

The percentage of U.S. AIDS cases attributed to heterosexual contact increased 21% from 1990 to 1991. [11]

Men who have sex with other men accounted for 48% of all new U.S. AIDS cases in 1993, down from 53% in 1992. [12]

Of the 339,250 AIDS cases reported in the United States between June 1981 and September 1993, 54% were attributed to men who have sex with other men (down from 61% as of 1989); 23% of the cases were attributed to intravenous drug use (up from 21% in 1989); and 7% of the cases were attributed to heterosexual contact. [13, 14]

In a 1991 survey of four communities (Dallas, Denver, Long Beach, and Seattle), 69%–90% of gay men (91% of them white) reported refraining from anal intercourse without a condom with anonymous partners. However, rates of HIV infection among African American and Latino gay men outside New York City, San Francisco, and Los Angeles were still increasing. [6, 15]

In a 1991 study of gay and bisexual men ages 17–22 who attended dance clubs in San Francisco and who consented to HIV testing, 12% were HIV positive; 14.3% of the Latino men and 22.9% of the African American men tested HIV positive. 43% of the men surveyed had recently engaged in unprotected anal intercourse. [16]

In California, gay men account for approximately 80% of all AIDS cases; yet less than 10% of the state's AIDS prevention funds are directed at the gay community. [17]

In a 1991 study by the National AIDS Behavior Society, more than 40% of Americans who engage in high-risk behaviors, most of whom were men who had had sex with other men within the last five years, had yet to be tested for HIV infection. [18]

In the United States, there were 79 reported cases of AIDS among lesbians as of 1989, representing 0.8% of all cases reported in adult women; 95% of the lesbians with AIDS are believed to have contracted HIV through intravenous drug use, 5% through tainted blood products. 80% were women of color. [19]

As of November 1993 there were 5 documented cases of female-to-female transmission of HIV. [20]

Two 1993 surveys of lesbian and bisexual women found that 47%–56.3% practiced unsafe sex. [21]

According to the Congressional Office of Technology Assessment, 86% of all insurers polled in 1991 required applicants for individual insurance to take HIV or other AIDS-related tests. [22]

25% of 561 hospitals surveyed in 1990 said they do not require a patient's consent before testing for HIV antibodies. [22]

As of 1991, all states required reporting of full-blown AIDS cases; 23 states also required reporting of HIV infection. [23]

42% of physicians surveyed by the American Medical Association in 1991 said HIV-positive patients were welcome in their practice. 75% were treating at least one HIV-positive person, while 83% said they lack sufficient information about AIDS. 35% said they would feel nervous among a group of homosexuals. [24]

More than 13,000 complaints of HIV-related discrimination were filed with state and local civil rights agencies between 1983 and 1988. 30% involved people who experienced discrimination because they cared for somebody with HIV disease or because of the perception that they were HIV infected. [25]

25 states have enacted laws criminalizing HIV transmission. [26]

More than 300 people have been prosecuted for allegedly putting others at risk of HIV transmission. About 50 of these cases resulted in convictions.[26]

The U.S. government has required HIV testing in four areas where it exercises control—in the military, in the Job Corps, in the Foreign Service, and in immigration—and has excluded, restricted, or expelled people who test positive for HIV antibodies. [25]

There is one AIDS-related death every twelve minutes in the United States. [7]

As of October 1993, 204,390 Americans had died of AIDS. The disease is the top killer of American men ages 25–44 and the fourth-leading killer of American women in the same age group. [13, 27]

In the United States between 1986 and 1992:
- Deaths from cancer increased 11%
- Deaths from heart disease decreased 6%
- Deaths from AIDS increased 201% [28, 29]

It is believed that AIDS deaths are underestimated by 25%. [30]

AIDS is the leading cause of death of young adults ages 25–44 in 64 U.S. cities. The 7 cities with the largest percentage of deaths from AIDS among this age group are as follows:
- San Francisco (61%)
- Elizabeth, New Jersey (51%)
- Fort Lauderdale (51%)
- Newark (45%)
- Miami (43%)
- Jersey City, New Jersey (43%)
- Seattle (39%) [30]

The 9 U.S. cities with the highest number of AIDS cases, in order of number of cases, are as follows:
- New York City
- Los Angeles
- San Francisco
- Miami
- Chicago
- Washington, D.C.
- Houston
- Newark
- Philadelphia [8]

For every case of HIV infection, the U.S. economy suffers a loss of $600,000 in medical costs and lost wages. [5, 31]

87% of Americans believe that "the government putting more money into AIDS research" would be an effective way to fight the epidemic. [5]

By the end of the 1990s the economic impact of HIV will reach at least $2.5 trillion. [5, 32]

3 in 4 people infected with HIV will end up in poverty. [5, 32]

SOURCES

1. John C. Gonsiorek and James D. Weinrich, eds., *Homosexuality: Research Implications for Public Policy*, Newbury Park, Calif.: Sage, 1991.
2. Vincent Price and Mei-Ling Hsu, "Public Opinion about AIDS Policies," *Public Opinion Quarterly*, Spring 1992.

3. World Health Organization, January 1993.
4. *San Francisco Chronicle,* July 20, 1992.
5. Gay Men's Health Crisis,"GMHC Facts," August 1993.
6. Jonathan Mann, Daniel J. M. Tarantola, and Thomas W. Weller, eds., *AIDS in the World,* Cambridge, Mass.: Harvard University Press, 1992.
7. Centers for Disease Control, January 1993.
8. Centers for Disease Control, October 1993.
9. *Newsday,* February 15, 1991.
10. Scott Williams, "AIDS Special Aimed at Teens," New York *Daily News,* August 28, 1992.
11. *CDC Quarterly HIV/AIDS Surveillance Report,* June 30, 1993.
12. Lauran Neergaard, "New Indicators Show AIDS #1 Killer of Men 25–44," Associated Press, October 28, 1993.
13. Centers for Disease Control National AIDS Hotline, 1993.
14. Jeffrey Schmalz, "Whatever Happened To AIDS?" *New York Times Magazine,* November 28, 1993.
15. A. Freeman et al., "Patterns of Sexual Behavior Change," *Journal of the American Medical Association* 266, December 25, 1991.
16. Karen Harbeck, ed., *Coming Out of the Classroom Closet: Gay and Lesbian Students, Teachers, and Curricula,* Binghamton, N.Y.: Harrington Park, 1992.
17. Jane Gross, "Second Wave of AIDS Feared by Officials in San Francisco," *New York Times,* December 11, 1993.
18. "Dossier," *The Advocate,* September 24, 1991.
19. *American Journal of Public Health* 80, November 1990.
20. New Jersey Women and AIDS Project, 1993.
21. Linda Wasowicz, "Study Finds High Rate of Risky AIDS Behavior among Lesbians," United Press International, October 19, 1993.
22. "News in Brief," *The Advocate,* January 15, 1991.
23. Tim Isaacks, "HIV Anonymity Battle Led by Colorado Researcher," *The Advocate,* February 12, 1991.
24. John Gallagher, "Survey Unearths AIDS-based Bias among Physicians," *The Advocate,* December 31, 1991.
25. Scott Buris, Harlon L. Dalton, Judith Leonie Miller, and the Yale AIDS Law Project, eds., *AIDS Law Today: A New Guide for the Public,* New Haven, Conn.: Yale University Press, 1993.
26. Scott R. Atkin, "States Crack Down on HIV Transmission," *The Advocate,* January 26, 1993.
27. "AIDS is the Top Killer Among Young Men," *New York Times,* October 31, 1993.
28. National Center for Health Statistics, 1993.
29. Centers for Disease Control, 1993.
30. Chris Bull, "Grim Reality," *The Advocate,* July 27, 1993.
31. *National Parents' Council on AIDS Spring Bulletin,* 1992.
32. Dr. James Mason, *Washington Journalism Review,* January/February 1992.

"Bisexuality was one of the most denied issues of the '80s. People bent over backwards to avoid the b word. . . . How would labels, assumptions, identities, and behaviors change if the bisexual community were a thriving recognized part of the lesbian and gay communities or if the bisexual movement were already an established and respected force among the many liberation movements?"

Lani Kaahumanu and Loraine Hutchins,
The Advocate, June 4, 1991

Statistical information on bisexuality is scarce. Bisexual issues are all too frequently omitted from studies of gay men and lesbians; this omission can often be attributed to "biphobia" within the gay community or to the pervasive myth that bisexuals do not really exist—they are in actuality gay men or lesbians unwilling to accept their same-sex attractions. The statistics in this section indicate that a significant portion of the population does indeed identify itself as bisexual. It further appears that research on bisexuality is increasing, although the reason appears not to be intrinsic interest in bisexuality but rather the fear that bisexuals will transmit AIDS within the heterosexual population.

Many antilesbian and antigay ballot measures, statutes, and policies include prohibitions against bisexuality. For example, Department of Defense Directive 1332.14 states that homosexuality and bisexuality are both incompatible with military service, while Colorado's Amendment Two was designed to forbid enactment of laws protecting bisexuals as well as gay men and lesbians. [1]

According to Alfred Kinsey, who constructed a seven-point scale to reflect the continuum of human sexual behavior, 50% of the men he studied could be classified as bisexual. [2]

Kinsey further reported that 18% of male subjects between the ages of 11 and 55 had demonstrated at least as much homosexual as heterosexual behavior during their lives and that 10% of married men participated in some homosexual activities. [3]

A 1974 cross-cultural study of male homosexuality in the United States, Holland, and Denmark found that 36%–59% of homosexual individuals studied (depending on the country) had had heterosexual intercourse. [4]

Two studies of lesbians from 1978 and 1989 found that 81% and 74% of those surveyed had engaged in heterosexual intercourse. [4]

In a 1985 study of bisexual women who were or had been married at the time of the survey:
- 47% were "somewhat aware" of their same-sex feelings before they were married
- 89% expressed sexual difficulties in their marriages
- 56% had had homosexual experiences during their marriages (24% of the husbands of those women knew about the relationships; 9% of the husbands approved)
- 20% tried to eliminate their homosexual feelings. [5]

In a 1985 study of couples in which the husband is bisexual and the wife is aware of it:
- the average length of the marriage was 13 years
- 69% of the males were aware of their homosexual feelings when they married
- 40% of the couples said the husband's homosexual behavior was known initially in the marriage
- 85% of the males and 76% of the females indicated they expected their marriage would be sexually open in the future
- 76% of the males and 78% of the females described their marriages as "outstanding" or "better than average." [3]

In a 1993 survey of self-identified bisexual men:
- 52% had both male and female partners within the past 6 months
- 3% belonged to lesbian and gay organizations
- 81% had read lesbian and gay papers or magazines
- 28% had attended local lesbian and gay pride parades
- 72% of their female spouses/lovers and 60–74% of family members knew nothing about their bisexuality. [6]

In the United States the first anthologies by and about bisexuals were published in 1990: *Bi Any Other Name: Bisexuals Speak Out* and *Bisexuality: A Reader and Sourcebook.*[7]

As of mid-1992 there were close to 350 organizations worldwide (roughly 80% of them located in the United States) that in some way addressed bisexual issues; 150 are college campus groups. [7]

SOURCES

1. *New York Times,* January 29, 1993.
2. Anastasia Toufexis, "Bisexuality: What Is It?" *Time,* August 17, 1992.
3. Timothy J. Wolf, "Marriages of Bisexual Men," *Journal of Homosexuality* 11 (nos. 1–2), 1985.
4. John C. Gonsiorek and James D. Weinrich, eds., *Homosexuality: Research Implications for Public Policy,* Newbury Park, Calif.: Sage, 1991.
5. Eli Coleman, "Bisexual Women in Marriages," *Journal of Homosexuality* 11 (nos. 1–2), 1985.
6. Joseph P. Stokes et al., "Sexual Behavior, Condom Use, Disclosure of Sexuality, and Stability of Sexual Orientation in Bisexual Men," *Journal of Sex Research* 30, August 1993.
7. Lily Braindrop, "Bi and Beyond," *The Advocate,* July 30, 1992.

"To hold that the act of homosexual sodomy is somehow protected as a fundamental right would be to cast aside millennia of moral teaching."

Chief Justice Warren Burger in *Bowers v. Hardwick*, 1986

The area of legal protections for lesbians and gay men is relatively easy to document for the simple reason that only a handful of states provide civil rights to lesbians and gay men. In most of the United States, it is entirely legal to deny employment, housing, or public accommodations to gay men or lesbians on the basis of their sexual orientation. In addition, there are dozens of laws that criminalize homosexual conduct, and an increasing number of ballot initiatives aimed at denying legal protections to lesbians and gay men.

SODOMY LAWS

Until 1961, every state had a sodomy law proscribing oral or anal sex between homosexuals and, in most cases, between heterosexuals. [1]

In 1948, Alfred Kinsey estimated that 95% of all American males were committing criminal sexual acts. [2]

In 1950, all but two states classified sodomy as a felony, with only murder, kidnapping, and rape commanding heavier sentences. [3]

The first state to decriminalize homosexuality was Illinois, in 1961. [4]

As of 1993, there were 20 states in which one could still be imprisoned for same-sex sexual relations, described as "sodomy," "unnatural intercourse," "deviate sexual conduct," "sexual misconduct," and "crimes against nature": Alabama, Arizona, Arkansas, Florida, Georgia, Idaho, Kansas, Maryland, Massachusetts, Minnesota, Mississippi, Missouri, Montana, North Carolina, Oklahoma, Rhode Island, South Carolina, Tennessee, Utah, and Virginia. [5]

4 states—Arkansas, Kansas, Missouri, and Tennessee—currently have laws that prohibit oral or anal sex only between persons of the same sex. [5]

Maximum penalties for sodomy convictions range from ten years in Oklahoma, North Carolina, Montana, Mississippi, and Maryland to life imprisonment in Idaho. The maximum penalty in Georgia, Rhode Island, and Virginia is 20 years. [6]

At least 150 lesbians and gay men were arrested in 1990 under seldom-enforced, often archaic laws used specifically against homosexuals. [7]

In two states—Louisiana and Texas—courts have struck down sodomy laws, with appeals pending before the state supreme court. In Kentucky and Michigan, state supreme courts have ruled sodomy laws unconstitutional. [5]

The repeal of Nevada's 82-year-old same-sex sodomy law in 1993 was the first undertaken by a state legislature since the 1986 U.S. Supreme Court ruling in *Bowers v. Hardwick.* [8]

Massachusetts enacted a gay rights law in 1990—even though its sodomy law was still on the books.[1]

Federal law prohibits sodomy among members of the military and in federal parks and buildings, even in states that have decriminalized sodomy. [9]

ANTIDISCRIMINATION STATUTES

As of September 1993, there were 140 ordinances, laws, or executive orders nationwide protecting the civil rights of lesbians and gay men. [6]

The first city to ban discrimination against gay men and lesbians was East Lansing, Michigan, in 1972. [4]

The first county to prohibit job discrimination against gay men and les-bians was Santa Cruz County in California, in 1975. [10]

The first law protecting gay and lesbian rights in a North American state or province was passed in 1977, by Quebec. [4]

The first state to pass a civil rights law protecting the rights of gay men and lesbians was Wisconsin, in 1982. [4]

Of 4,000 bias complaints filed in Wisconsin in 1992, 100 alleged antigay or antilesbian discrimination.[11]

The first bill to extend federal civil rights protection to gay men and lesbians was introduced in Congress on May 14, 1974. No federal civil rights law has yet been enacted. [10]

8 states have laws passed by the legislature and signed by the governor protecting gay and lesbian rights: California, Connecticut, Hawaii, Massachusetts, Minnesota, New Jersey, Vermont, and Wisconsin. [6]

71 cities or counties have civil rights ordinances protecting lesbians and gay men. [6]

45 cities and counties have council or mayoral proclamations banning discrimination against lesbians and gays in public employment. [6]

ANTIGAY LEGISLATION

In 1992 elections, two states (Colorado and Oregon) and two cities (Tampa and Portland, Maine) put antigay measures before the voters. The Colorado and Tampa measures passed by margins of 53% to 47% and 58% to 42%, respectively. The Oregon and Portland measures were defeated by margins of 56% to 44% and 57% to 43%, respectively. (The Colorado measure was subsequently challenged as unconstitutional.) [12]

In 1993 elections, 3 cities—Cincinnati; Lewiston, Maine; and Portsmouth, New Hampshire—passed antigay measures by margins of 61% to 31%, 70% to 30%, and 60% to 40%, respectively. [6]

From November 3, 1992, to September 30, 1993, at least 132 attempts to restrict the rights of gay men and lesbians occurred in 41 states and the District of Columbia. This activity included statewide ballot initiatives, legislative battles, state court decisions, local ordinances, curriculum controversies, and attempts at censorship. [13]

9 states are facing efforts to place antigay and antilesbian initiatives on the November 1994 ballot: Arizona, California, Florida, Idaho, Maine, Michigan, Missouri, Oregon, and Washington. 7 of the 9 states have witnessed direct involvement by national or religious right groups. [13]

Lesbians and gay men have virtually no legal rights when a partner becomes incapacitated because of accident or illness. [6]

In the past 35 years, there have been more than a dozen major actions by the U.S. Supreme Court on gay and lesbian issues. Among the major decisions are the following:

- In 1958, in *One Inc. v. Olessen* the Court overturned a California district court order banning distribution of *One,* a gay magazine, through the mail
- In 1967, the Court voted 6-3 in *Boutilier v. Immigration and Naturalization Service* that the Immigration and Naturalization Service could legally exclude homosexuals from entering the United States
- In 1976, the Court voted 6-3 not to hear an appeal in *Doe v. Commonwealth's Attorney,* thereby upholding a Virginia court's ruling that there is no constitutional right to engage in private homosexual activity
- In 1976, in *Enslin v. North Carolina* the Court upheld the conviction of a Jacksonville, North Carolina, man sentenced to one year in prison for having oral sex with a consenting male partner in the privacy of his home
- In 1986, the Court voted 5-4 in *Bowers v. Hardwick* to uphold the constitutionality of Georgia's sodomy laws. [14]

As of 1992, at least 41% of the 41 female inmates on death row in the United States were lesbians. [15]

SOURCES

1. William B. Rubenstein, *Lesbians, Gay Men and the Law,* New York: The New Press, 1993.
2. John C. Gonsiorek and James D. Weinrich, eds., *Homosexuality: Research Implications for Public Policy,* Newbury Park, Calif.: Sage, 1991.
3. Gary David Comstock, *Violence against Lesbians and Gay Men,* New York: Columbia University Press, 1991.
4. Lynne Yamaguchi Fletcher, *The First Gay Pope and Other Records,* Boston: Alyson, 1992.
5. Lambda Legal Defense and Education Fund Inc., New York, 1993.
6. National Gay and Lesbian Task Force, Washington, D.C., 1993.
7. Dell Richards, "Activism = Arrests," *The Advocate,* April 9, 1991.
8. John Gallagher, "Jackpot," *The Advocate,* July 27, 1993.
9. Arthur S. Leonard, "Report from the Legal Front," *The Nation,* July 2, 1990.
10. Leigh W. Rutledge, *The Gay Decades: From Stonewall to the Present, the People and Events That Shaped Gay Lives,* New York: Plume, 1992.
11. Joseph P. Shapiro et al., "Straight Talk about Gays," *U. S. News and World Report,* July 5, 1993.
12. John Gallagher, "A New Attitude," *The Advocate,* December 1, 1992.
13. *Hostile Climate: A State by State Report on Anti-gay Activities,* New York: People For the American Way, 1993.
14. Leigh Rutledge, *The Gay Fireside Companion,* Boston: Alyson, 1989.
15. Masha Gessen, "The Year in Review," *The Advocate,* January 12, 1993.

"Like most scientific discourse, research on homosexuality has been filtered through societal biases. Among its other effects, this has meant that white, middle-class and above all, adult, English-speaking males have been studied more than their numbers warrant."

John C. Gonsiorek and James D. Weinrich,
Homosexuality: Research Implications for Public Policy, 1991

Unlike women or racial minorities, lesbians and gay men are not measured by the U.S. census, making it extremely difficult to obtain accurate demographic information on the gay and lesbian community. Further, information that is available has become a double-edged sword, since the religious right has argued that lesbians and gay men have no need for civil rights protections, given their privileged socioeconomic status. The closest approximation to a "lesbian and gay census" has emerged in studies conducted by Overlooked Opinions, a Chicago polling organization that has done pioneering work in ascertaining demographic data on gay and lesbian Americans.

DEMOGRAPHICS
The fifteen largest concentrations of the lesbian and gay population in the United States are:

1. Manhattan
2. San Francisco
3. Boston/Cambridge
4. Seattle
5. Oakland/Berkeley
6. Washington, D.C.
7. Chicago/Evanston
8. Atlanta
9. Minneapolis
10. Marin County, California
11. Los Angeles
12. Santa Monica Bay
13. Portland
14. San Diego
15. Pittsburgh [1]

Of all lesbians and gay men, 45.1% and 52.7% live in urban areas, respectively, while 33.1% and 31.7% live in the suburbs, respectively. [2]

10% of the population of California is lesbian or gay, constituting 12.1% of the lesbian and gay population of the United States; 27.6% of the population of San Francisco is lesbian or gay. [2]

Of the 3,187,772 "unmarried partners" counted in the 1990 U.S. census, it was inadvertently discovered that 145,130 are same-sex couples. There were 9,301 in New York City, 6,816 in San Francisco, 3,842 in Chicago, and 2,213 in Washington, D.C. (Census officials admit that these figures do not reflect the true number of same-sex couples living together.) [3, 4]

As of 1989, an estimated 15,000 to 20,000 postoperative male-to-female transsexuals resided in the United States. [5]

82% of the lesbians and 69% of the gay men who voted in the 1992 presidential election had some college training, versus 66% of all women and 67% of all men who voted. [6]

In a 1992 survey of 7,500 lesbians and gay men, Overlooked Opinions found the following: [2, 7]

	Lesbians	Gay Men	National
Registered to vote (of those eligible) (%)	90.0	92.9	68.2
Voted in the 1988 presidential election (%)	82.0	87.9	61.3
Democrat (%)	66.7	62.0	48.7*
Independent (%)	21.3	19.5	13.3*
Republican (%)	6.8	13.1	33.8*
Other party affiliation (%)	5.2	5.4	4.2*

36% of lesbian and gay Americans live in households earning $50,000 or more, and 7% live in households earning $100,000 or more. [8]

The average household income for lesbians in the United States is estimated at $45,927, while the average household income for gay men is estimated at $51,325. In 1990, average household income in the United States was $36,520. [2, 9]

Men account for two of every three dollars spent by lesbian and gay consumers. [8]

Some 43% of lesbians and 48% of gay men own their own home. [2]

Between 1988 and 1991, lesbians and gay men bought 5,925,000 home computers. [2]

Lesbians and gay men took more than 162 million trips in 1991, 127 million of which were on business. [2]

---

* These figures are based on data compiled in the 30 states that tabulate voters' party affiliation.

In 1988, 73% of gay men and lesbians took at least one airline trip, versus a national average of 17.4%. [10]

SOCIAL ACTIVITIES/RECREATION

81% of gay men have dined out more than 5 times in the past month. [2]

15% of lesbians own four or more cats or dogs. [2]

65% of lesbians go camping. [2]

1,300 gay and lesbian athletes participated in the 1982 Gay Games; 3,482 took part in the 1986 Gay Games; 7,016 competed in the 1990 Gay Games. Organizers expect 15,000 athletes to take part in the 31 sports scheduled for Gay Games IV in June of 1994. [11]

1 in 5 gay men go to a health club ten times or more per month. [2]

According to *Bob Damron's Address Book* (1993), there are 1,672 lesbian and gay bars in the United States. [12]

The percentage of homosexuals who go to gay and lesbian bars with any frequency is estimated at between 10% and 25%. [13]

SOURCES

1. Raymond G. McLeod, "Gay Market a Potential Goldmine," *San Francisco Chronicle,* August 27, 1991.
2. Overlooked Opinions, Inc., Chicago, Illinois, 1993.
3. "San Francisco is Really For Lovers," *Bay Area Reporter,* September 16, 1993.
4. U.S. Census Bureau, Department of Marriage and Family, Washington D.C., 1993.
5. Leigh W. Rutledge, *The Gay Fireside Companion,* Boston: Alyson, 1989.
6. Anne Cronin, "Two Viewfinders, Two Pictures of Gay America," *New York Times,* June 27, 1993.
7. *Voting and Registration in the Election of 1992,* U.S. Department of Commerce and Statistics Administration, Bureau of the Census, Washington D.C., 1993.
8. "The Gay Market," *Affluent Marketers Alert* IV, March 1992.
9. Pringle Pipkin, "Advertisers Discovering Gay Market," *Kansas City Star,* May 10, 1992.
10. Kathy Seal, "Gay Travel and Accommodations Increase," *Hotel and Motel Management,* December 17, 1990.
11. Steve Tracy, "Good Sports," *The Advocate,* August 14, 1990.
12. Bob Damron, *The 29th Edition of Bob Damron's Address Book,* San Francisco: Damron, 1993.
13. John C. Gonsiorek and James D. Weinrich, eds., *Homosexuality: Research Implications for Public Policy,* Newbury Park, Calif.: Sage, 1991.

"If we define the nuclear family as a working husband, housekeeping wife, and two children, and ask how many Americans still live in this type of family, the answer is astonishing: seven percent of the total United States population."

Alvin Toffler

Lamentably, it appears that many in powerful positions, such as the Virginia judge who in 1993 declared a lesbian mother "unfit" to retain custody of her son, are unaware of or unwilling to accept the research done on gay and lesbian families and relationships. The facts go far in debunking myths that cast gay men and lesbians as unsuitable parents or as "recruiters" determined to persuade unsuspecting children to choose the "homosexual lifestyle." Furthermore, despite the ban on same-sex marriage, a large portion of the community are in fact in committed relationships.

RELATIONSHIPS

3 of 4 lesbians surveyed between 1978 and 1980 were in steady relationships. [1]

In studies conducted between 1977 and 1983, 40%–60% of gay men interviewed were in steady relationships. [1]

In a 1992 study, 55.5% of gay men and 71.2% of lesbians were in steady relationships. [2]

Of the 1,266 lesbian and gay couples that took part in a 1988 survey conducted by Partners Task Force for Gay and Lesbian Couples:

- On the average, the couples had been together for 6 years
- More than 80% had been together for more than 1 year
- The most frequent way in which lesbians met one another was through friends (28%); meeting through work was second (21%)
- The most frequent meeting place for men was a bar (22%); meeting through friends ranked second (19%)
- 87% of the women and 93% of the men lived together
- Less than 10% were unsatisfied with their sexual relationships. [3]

In a 1982 study of lesbians in couples:
- 90% agreed that both partners should have equal say in the relationship
- 45% agreed that both parties do have equal say in the relationship
- 55% perceived a power imbalance in the relationship
- 17% indicated that both partners initiated sex to exactly the same degree. [4]

In a 1987 study of gay male couples:
- 45% of the partners reported no previous relationship
- 40.7% met at a bar
- Finances was the biggest conflict reported (39.3%); family members were the next highest source of conflict (22.5%)
- 96.4% said they were monogamous. [5]

In 1981, no public or private jurisdiction in the United States recognized lesbian or gay relationships. [6]

As of September 1993, 25 jurisdictions recognized some sort of domestic partnership for lesbians and gay men. [7]

In October 1993 New York City became the thirteenth municipal government to extend health benefits to domestic partners, both same-sex and opposite-sex. [8]

At least 20 private-sector companies and organizations recognize same-sex domestic partnerships in employee benefits. [7]

As of November 1993, all 50 states denied gay men and lesbians the right to marry. [7]

The state supreme court of Hawaii has stated that prohibiting same-sex marriage may violate that state's equal protection statutes. [9]

The largest mass wedding of lesbians and gay men—involving more than 3,000 couples—took place at the third National March on Washington on April 24, 1993. [10]

FAMILY

There are currently between 1 million and 5 million lesbian mothers in the United States and between 1 million and 3 million gay fathers. [11]

An estimated 6 million to 14 million children have a lesbian or gay parent. [11]

An estimated 10,000 children are being raised by lesbians who became pregnant through artificial insemination. [12]

35 studies conducted in the last 15 years have shown that the children of gay and lesbian parents are no more likely to become homosexuals than children of heterosexuals and are just as well adjusted. [13]

A review of 9 studies of aspects of personal development—such as self-concept, moral judgment, and intelligence—revealed no significant difference between children of lesbians and gay men and children of heterosexuals. [11]

New Hampshire has a law expressly prohibiting lesbians and gay men from adopting children. It also bars lesbians and gay men from becoming foster parents. [7]

While 6 states permit joint adoption by same-sex couples, most adoptions by lesbian or gay couples are officially recorded as single-parent adoptions. [7, 14]

11 states have laws that make sexual orientation irrelevant in custody cases. [7]

Courts in 11 states have ruled that gay men and lesbians, on the basis of their sexual orientation, are unfit to receive custody of their children. [7]

In 17 states, courts have ruled that sexual orientation can be a factor in child-custody decisions only if a connection is made between the parent's sexual orientation and an adverse impact on the child. [15]

9 states have no published decisions on lesbian and gay child custody. [15]

SOURCES

1. John C. Gonsiorek and James D. Weinrich, eds., *Homosexuality: Research Implications for Public Policy,* Newbury Park, Calif.: Sage, 1991.
2. Overlooked Opinions, "The Gay Market," Chicago, January 1992.
3. Partners Task Force for Gay and Lesbian Couples, "Survey of Gay Couples," Seattle, 1990.
4. Mary Ellen Reilly and Jean M. Lynch, "Power Sharing in Lesbian Relationships," *Journal of Homosexuality* 19 (no. 3), 1990.
5. Raymond M. Berger, "Men Together: Understanding the Gay Couple," *Journal of Homosexuality* 19 (no. 3), 1990.
6. William B. Rubenstein, *Lesbians, Gay Men, and the Law,* New York: The New Press, 1993.
7. National Gay and Lesbian Task Force, Washington, D.C., 1993.
8. Celia W. Dugger, "Workers' Partners Added to Health Plan by Dinkins," *New York Times,* October 31, 1993.
9. John Leo, "Gay Rights, Gay Marriages," *U.S. News and World Report,* May 24, 1993.
10. "Universal Fellowship of Metropolitan Community Churches Fact Sheet, " 1993.
11. Charlotte J. Patterson, "Children of Lesbian and Gay Parents," *Child Development* 63, 1992.
12. Bill Turque et al., "Gays Under Fire," *Newsweek,* September 14, 1992.
13. Jane Gross, "New Challenge of Youth: Growing Up in Gay Home," *New York Times,* February 11, 1991.
14. "Mother Files to Bar Adoption by Gay Couple," *New York Times,* September 20, 1993.
15. National Center for Lesbian Rights, San Francisco, 1993.

"A homosexual is after all a human being..."

Federal District Judge Philip Neville, 1970

Deep-seated homophobia still exists within the health and medicine fields. One cause of this homophobia may be lack of information: statistics indicate that gay issues receive little attention in the education of health professionals. It further appears that the health needs of the gay and lesbian community are vastly undermet, as many lesbians and gay men are reluctant to reveal their sexual orientation to their health providers. And while AIDS has understandably emerged as a dominant health issue in the gay and lesbian community, many other issues merit increased research and attention, including alcoholism and domestic violence.

In 1942, the American Psychiatric Association declared that homosexuality is a disease. [1]

In 1973, the American Psychiatric Association removed homosexuality from its list of diseases. The next year, 37% of its membership voted to reclassify homosexuality as a disease; they were not successful. [1,2]

According to the American Psychological Association, no scientific evidence exists to support the effectiveness of any of the therapies that attempt to convert homosexuals to heterosexuals. [1]

In a 1989 survey of all counselor education programs in the country, fewer than 10% of counselors were required to take a course in sexuality. [3]

In a 1989 survey of doctoral programs approved by the American Psychological Association, 37% offered a graduate course in human sexuality. [3]

In a 1989 study of 100 nurses teaching in nursing programs:
- 52% thought lesbianism is unnatural
- 34% thought lesbians are "disgusting"
- 20% thought lesbians transmit AIDS
- 17% thought lesbians molest children. [4]

In a 1986 study of 1,009 physicians in San Diego:
- 40% were uncomfortable treating lesbians and gay men
- 30% opposed admitting lesbians and gay men into medical school
- 40% would not refer patients to a lesbian or gay colleague. [4]

In a 1991 survey of four-year medical schools in the United States, the mean amount of course time devoted to the topic of homosexuality was 3 hours, 26 minutes. [5]

In a 1988 study of lesbians' relationships with their health-care providers, 72% recounted negative experiences. [6]

A 1988 study of 529 African American lesbians and bisexuals found that only 33% had disclosed their sexual orientation to their health-care provider. [4]

In a 1989 health-care study of 1,681 Michigan lesbians, 6% had a health-care provider who was lesbian or gay, 61% felt they were unable to come out to their provider, and 6% of their providers tried to "cure" their patients' lesbianism. [7]

Some 77% of lesbians and gay men prefer medical facilities with gay-specific programs. [8]

It is estimated that 1 in 3 lesbians are at increased risk for breast cancer as a result of not bearing children by age 30 and because of high incidences of weight and alcohol problems. [9]

In three studies conducted between 1986 and 1989, it was found that 9%–19% of gay men and lesbians in the United States are alcoholics. The Department of Health and Human Services estimates that 10% of the general U.S. population are alcoholics. [10, 11]

In a 1985 study of gay men recovering from alcoholism, 100% reported denying their homosexuality while drinking; 90% reported accepting their homosexuality when they achieved sobriety. [12]

Domestic violence is the third-largest health problem facing gay men today, second only to substance abuse and AIDS. [13]

Between 350,000 and 650,000 gay men in the United States are victims of domestic violence perpetrated by their lovers. [13]

According to Women Inc., a San Francisco–based organization serving battered women, domestic violence occurs in 1 in 4 lesbian relationships—roughly the same percentage as in heterosexual relationships. [14]

More than 50% of lesbians surveyed at the 1985 Michigan women's music festival reported being abused by their female partner. Half of the women reporting abuse admitted that they had perpetrated abuse on a partner. [15]

It was estimated in 1991 that a total of no more than 20 professionals scattered in 4 American cities are adequately experienced or trained to deal effectively with lesbian and gay victims of domestic violence. [13]

SOURCES

1. John C. Gonsiorek and James D. Weinrich, eds., *Homosexuality: Research Implications for Public Policy,* Newbury Park, Calif.: Sage, 1991.
2. David Gelman, "Born or Bred?" *Newsweek,* February 24, 1992.
3. Karen M. Harbeck, *Coming Out of the Classroom Closet: Gay and Lesbian Students, Teachers, and Curricula,* Binghamton, N.Y.: Harrington Park, 1992.
4. Patricia E. Stevens, "Lesbian Health Care Research: A Review of the Literature from 1970 to 1990," *Health Care for Women International* 13, 1992.
5. Molly M. Wallick et al., "How the Topic of Homosexuality Is Taught at U.S. Medical Schools," *Academic Medicine* 67, September 1992.
6. P. E. Stevens and J. M. Hall, "Stigma, Health Beliefs and Experiences with Health Care in Lesbian Women," *Image: Journal of Nursing Scholarship* 20 (no. 2), 1988.
7. *Michigan Organization for Human Rights Report,* August 1991.
8. Overlooked Opinions, Inc., Chicago, 1993.
9. Masha Gessen, "Lesbians and Breast Cancer, " *The Advocate,* February 9, 1993.
10. Felicia E. Halpert, "Sobering Thoughts," *Essence,* November 1991.
11. Jay P. Paul et al., "Gay and Alcoholic: Epidemiologic and Clinical Issues," *Alcohol Health and Research World* 15 (no. 2), 1991.
12. Robert J. Kus, "Alcoholism and Non-acceptance of Gay Self: The Critical Link," *Journal of Homosexuality* 15 (nos. 1–2), 1988.
13. David Island, *Men Who Beat the Men Who Love Them: Battered Gay Men and Domestic Violence,* Binghamton, N.Y.: Harrington Park, 1991.
14. Women Inc., San Francisco, 1993.
15. Gwat-Yong Lie and Sabrina Gentlewarrier, "Intimate Violence in Lesbian Relationships: Discussion of Survey Findings and Practice Implications," *Journal of Social Service Research* 15 (nos. 1–2), 1991.

"During the last ten years the number of developing countries and former Communist countries with gay and lesbian movements has grown impressively."

The Third Pink Book: A Global View of Lesbian and Gay Liberation and Oppression

A look at lesbian and gay issues in an international context reveals several countries with legislation more tolerant than in the United States and scores whose laws are less progressive. While rumors and allegations of abuses of lesbians and gay men in the international arena are pervasive, it is extremely difficult to confirm or quantify such reports. Neither Amnesty International nor the International Lesbian and Gay Association (ILGA), a worldwide federation of more than 300 lesbian and gay groups in 50 nations, can provide concrete numbers of gay political prisoners abroad or hard data on enforcement of sodomy laws. On the other hand, ILGA has made groundbreaking efforts in targeting areas in which progress has been made and in assembling an up-to-date data base of information on international laws related to lesbians and gay men. Much of the information in this section is derived from ILGA's definitive publication, *The Third Pink Book: A Global View of Lesbian and Gay Liberation and Oppression.*

Homosexual acts between consenting adults were decriminalized in France in 1810, in Russia in 1917, in Poland in 1932, in Switzerland in 1942, in Spain in 1980, and in New Zealand in 1986. Russia recriminalized homosexual acts in 1934. [1]

In July 1993, ILGA became the first and only lesbian and gay group to be recognized by the United Nations. [2]

Of the 202 countries examined in ILGA's *Third Pink Book*:
- Some form of lesbian and gay movement exists in 56 countries
- Lesbian and gay rights groups are in formation in 15 countries
- There is no known gay group or movement in 131 countries
- A majority of the population favors equal rights for lesbians and gays in 11 countries
- A minority of the population favors equal rights for lesbians and gays in 47 countries

- There is hardly any public support of equal rights for lesbians and gay men in 144 countries
- Laws protect lesbians and gay men against discrimination in 6 countries (and in some parts of the United States, Canada, and Australia)
- 98 countries do not criminalize homosexual acts, but there is no protection against discrimination on the basis of sexual orientation
- 24 countries have no information available on the legal status of lesbians and gays. [3]

Of the 74 countries with laws prohibiting homosexual behavior, 72% are predominantly Islamic, formerly Communist, or previously part of the British Empire. [3]

Penalties for homosexual acts range from ten days' imprisonment (Ethiopia) to a fine of 25 rupees and/or a beating with laths outside the police station (India) to life imprisonment (Guyana). In eight countries in which Islamic law applies, men who commit homosexual acts can be sentenced to death. [3]

In 23 of the 74 countries in which men can be punished for homosexual acts, women are not mentioned in the laws. [3]

According to official records, between 50,000 and 63,000 males, including 4,000 juveniles, were convicted of homosexuality in Germany between 1933 and 1944. [4]

The estimated number of gay men exterminated during the Third Reich ranges from 10,000 to 1,000,000; 220,000 is one of the most frequently cited numbers. [5]

Unlike Jews, political prisoners, and other groups of survivors of the concentration camps, none of the homosexual inmates who survived Nazi camps was granted any compensation. [4]

Amnesty International debated for 17 years before classifying persecuted gays as prisoners of conscience in 1991. [6]

In Russia 30% of the population is in favor of lesbian and gay rights; 33% is in favor of killing homosexuals. [3]

Before the dissolution of the Soviet Union, an average of 700 men were jailed each year for being gay. [6]

Since Lithuania regained its independence in 1990, 7 men (including 1 minor) have been sentenced to 3 to 8 years' imprisonment for same-sex acts. [3]

In 1990, the Czech gay rights group Lambda Praha had 171 members, including 20 women. [6]

In Austria, male and female homosexual acts were decriminalized in 1971, and homosexual prostitution was legalized in 1989. Yet Section 220 of the penal code provides for up to six months' imprisonment or a fine for those who "advocate or promote homosexuality (both male and female) or bestiality." [3]

In a 1991 Gallup Poll in Britain:
- 49% believed there were more gays now than twenty years ago
- 53% considered homosexuality an acceptable "alternative lifestyle"
- 66% believed same-sex acts should be legal. [7]

In Britain, homosexual acts between two consenting adults were decriminalized in 1967. Until 1992, being homosexual was a bar to appointment to senior civil service and diplomatic positions. [3]

Gay bashing in London rose 350% in 1989. [6]

In 1992 the Court of Appeals of London upheld the convictions of 5 men found guilty of sadomasochistic sex with consenting adults and sentenced the men to up to four-and-a-half years in prison. [3]

The Congo Embassy in Brussels stated on April 13, 1987, that "the practice of homosexuality does not exist in the Congo." [3]

Sexual activity between adult males is illegal in South Africa. Pornography is also outlawed.[8]

However, in November 1993, the main political parties in South Africa endorsed a new constitution that includes a provision forbidding discrimination based on sexual orientation. [9]

The greater Johannesburg-Soweto lesbian and gay group GLOW, founded in 1988, has nearly 400 members, 60% of whom are black. [8]

There have been 12 targeted murders of lesbian and gay activists in Mexico within the last year. [10]

Nicaraguan law stipulates 1 to 3 years' imprisonment of any individual who "induces, promotes, propagandizes or practices in a scandalous manner sexual intercourse between people of the same sex." [3]

In Chile, lesbian and gay groups exist but are illegal. There is also a policy of compulsory HIV testing of all gay men. [3]

Although at least a minority of the population is in favor of gay and lesbian rights in Brazil, more than 320 lesbians and gays were reported recently killed in the state of Bahia because of their sexual orientation. [3]

The Japan International Lesbian and Gay Association, founded in 1984 with 2 members, now has 300 members. Of these, only 8 are out. [11]

In China, being lesbian or gay is considered not a sin but an illness and is treated with shock therapy or emetics. [12]

Tasmania is the only Australian state in which sexual acts between men are still illegal. Sexual acts between women are not mentioned in the law. [3]

In Sydney, Australia, 32% of nondomestic homicides in 1991 were antigay murders. [13]

In Canada, sodomy and anal intercourse between consenting adults 18 years or older were eliminated as offenses in 1988. [3]

In 1993, 55% of the Canadian population found homosexuality morally acceptable. [14]

In 1986, Denmark recognized lesbian and gay couples in inheritance tax legislation. In 1987 sexual orientation was added to the antidiscrimination clause in the penal code. [3]

Denmark and Norway are the only two countries that allow lesbian and gay couples to marry. [3]

In the Netherlands, 90% of the population is in favor of equal rights for lesbians and gays.[3]

SOURCES

1. Leigh W. Rutledge, *The Gay Book of Lists,* Boston: Alyson, 1987.
2. Duncan Osborne, "The Trouble with NAMBLA," *The Advocate,* December 14, 1993.
3. Aart Hendriks, Rob Tielman, and Evert van der Veen, *The Third Pink Book: A Global View of Lesbian and Gay Liberation and Oppression,* Buffalo, N.Y.: Prometheus, 1993.
4. Richard Plante, *The Pink Triangle,* New York: Holt, 1986.
5. Frank Rector, *The Nazi Extermination of Homosexuals,* New York: Stein & Day, 1981.
6. Kate Krauss, *Out/Look,* Winter 1992.
7. "International News in Brief," *The Advocate,* November 19, 1991.
8. Neil Miller, *Out in the World,* New York: Random House, 1992.
9. Bill Keller, "South African Parties Endorse Constitution Granting Rights to All," *New York Times,* November 18, 1993.
10. "Amnesty International Takes Up Gay and Lesbian Oppression," Reuters News Service, October 24, 1993.
11. John Storey, "Taking on Tokyo," *The Advocate,* October 20, 1992.
12. Nicholas D. Kristof, "China Using Electrodes to 'Cure' Homosexuals," *New York Times,* January 29, 1990.
13. Margaret Kwasniewska, "Fun and Fear in Sydney," *The Advocate,* March 10, 1992.
14. "Agenda," *The Advocate,* May 18, 1993.

"Yes, out gays and lesbians have hit mainstream entertainment with a vengeance."

Pier Carlo Talenti, *The Advocate 1993 Fall Preview*

Gay men and lesbians are now national news. The debate over gays and lesbians in the military, though unsuccessful in overturning the Pentagon's ban, did catapult gay and lesbian issues onto the front pages of the nation's daily newspapers and weekly news magazines. And whereas early gay rights demonstrations received little or no coverage, the 1993 March on Washington garnered extensive attention in print and visual media alike. At the same time, gay and lesbian visibility is on the rise in Hollywood, while the lesbian and gay publishing industry is setting new records for profits as more readers than ever are buying books and magazines on gay and lesbian issues.

Of the 11,339 newspapers in the United States in 1991, 125 were gay and lesbian oriented, with a combined total circulation exceeding 1 million. [1]

The *Bay Area Reporter,* a San Francisco weekly with a circulation of 37,000, is the most highly circulated gay weekly in the United States. [2]

In May 1992, Deb Price of the *Detroit News* began writing the first nationally syndicated weekly column devoted to lesbian and gay issues. [3]

The *New York Times* first allowed the word "gay" to be used as a synonym for "homosexual" in July 1987. [4]

In a 1992 survey of senior editors of American newspapers, 77% thought their coverage of lesbian and gay issues was fair or poor, while 70% thought their coverage of AIDS was good or excellent. [5]

In a 1990 sample of gay men and lesbians who work at newspapers:
- 59% said they are "out" at work but that they believe the large majority of gay and lesbian journalists are closeted
- 81% had heard derogatory comments about gay men and lesbians in general at their newspaper within the last year

- nearly 9 of 10 said being gay or lesbian made no difference in the quality of assignments they received
- 83% of "out" newspaper workers said they have not been approached by managers for advice on gay-related workplace issues within the last six months. [6]

The first known gay periodical was *Urnings,* published in 1870 in Germany by Karl Heinrich Ulrichs. There was only one issue. [2]

The first wide-circulation gay periodical in North America was *One Magazine: The Homosexual Viewpoint,* first published in 1953. [2]

The Advocate has the largest circulation of any lesbian or gay periodical in the United States, with 95,000–100,00 readers for each biweekly issue. [2]

98% of the readers of *The Advocate* are men. [7]

Of the 41 entries listed under "Gay Men" in the General Periodical Archive of the InfoTrac data base for 1980 to 1985, 39 are related to disease. [8]

As of 1993, the *Reader's Guide to Periodical Literature* had refused to index a single lesbian or gay magazine, despite having recently added 20 new periodicals, including *Vanity Fair.* The most frequently cited publication among the guide's 1991 listings on AIDS was *Vogue.* [9]

In 1993, Amanda Bearse of the television comedy *Married . . . With Children* became the first prime-time series actor to come out of the closet. [10]

At least 6 prime-time television series have featured a recurring gay or lesbian character: *Soap, Dynasty, Hot L Baltimore, Roseanne, Melrose Place,* and *Heartbeat.* [2]

The first gay characters to appear regularly on television were Gordon and George of *Hot L Baltimore,* on ABC in 1975. [2]

The first lesbian character to appear regularly on a prime-time television series was Marilyn McGrath of *Heartbeat* on ABC in 1989. [2]

Out There, the first "all-queer" comedy special, was broadcast December 3, 1993, on the Comedy Central cable network. [11]

Journal Graphics' *Sex and Sexuality Index* lists 1,027 television and radio programs with gay or lesbian themes that aired on CNN, PBS, NPR, and in syndication. Of these, 151 were broadcast between 1982 and 1989; 876 aired between 1990 and 1993. [12]

This Way Out, a gay and lesbian radio program that began in 1988, is broadcast on 85 radio stations in 6 countries. [13]

Mart Crowley's 1968 play *The Boys in the Band* played for exactly 1,000 performances off-Broadway at Theater Four. [14]

The 1993 edition of *Gay and Lesbian American Plays: An Annotated Bibliography* lists nearly 700 plays with lesbian and gay themes. [15]

Of the more than 400 films listed in the *Gay Hollywood Film and Video Guide:*
- 44 have gay characters that are murderers or victims of murder
- 48 have gay characters that are "sissies" or other stereotypes
- 69 have gay characters that are drag queens
- 12 have gay characters that are either Fascists or Nazis
- 4 have gay characters that are vampires
- 5 have gay characters that are heroes or are happy. [16]

Of the 73 lesbian and gay film festivals worldwide (32 in the United States), the San Francisco International Lesbian and Gay Film Festival is the largest and oldest, dating from 1977, when a one-night showing drew around 200 people. San Francisco's 1993 festival was attended by approximately 52,000 people. [17]

Marlon Riggs's film *Tongues Untied,* a documentary about African American gay men which was funded in part by a grant from the National Endowment for the Arts (NEA), was the subject of 13 formal complaints to the Federal Communications Commission. [18]

In July of 1991, the NEA bowed to pressure from Congress and denied grants totaling $23,000 to four performance artists, Karen Finley, John Fleck, Holly Hughes, and Tim Miller, whose work deals frankly with lesbian and gay issues and gender politics. [19]

In the United States, from November 1992 to September 1993, there were at least 14 attempts by religious right groups to ban books because of their discussion of homosexuality. [20]

In a survey of 35,000 gay men, 82% said reading was a favorite hobby. [21]

In the United States, as of May 1991, there were 105 small- to medium-sized publishers of lesbian- and gay-related books. [22]

As of April 1991 there were 60 lesbian- or gay-operated archives and community libraries in the United States. [22]

In 1977, there were 8 gay and lesbian bookstores in the United States. Today, there are 186 bookstores and mail-order firms in 41 states and the District of Columbia specializing in lesbian, gay, and feminist books. [21, 22]

In 1991 there were 106 feminist bookstores in the United States and Canada, with sales of $31 million; 40% of those sales were for lesbian books. [21]

At Chicago's Unabridged Books, lesbian and gay titles make up 10% of the stock but account for up to 33% of the sales. [23]

The national average of sales per square foot in bookstores is $300. At gay and lesbian bookstores in Washington, D.C., and New York City, sales per square foot are nearly 4 times the national average. [21]

A Different Light bookstore in San Francisco recorded a 12%–14% increase in sales for the first four months of 1993 and a 20% increase in May 1993. [24]

The first collection of black gay writers was *In the Life*, edited by Joseph Beam and published by Alyson Publications in 1986. [25]

4 books on gay and lesbian issues made it onto national and regional bestseller lists in the first half of 1993: Randy Shilts's *Conduct Unbecoming: Gays and Lesbians in the U.S. Military;* Michaelangelo Signorile's *Queer in America: Sex, the Media and the Closets of Power;* Martin Duberman's *Stonewall;* and Frank Browning's *The Culture of Desire.* [24]

SOURCES

1. Jonathan Curiel, "Gay Newspapers," *Editor and Publisher,* August 3, 1991.
2. Lynne Yamaguchi Fletcher, *The First Gay Pope and Other Records,* Boston: Alyson, 1992.
3. John Purnell, "All the (Gay) News That's Fit to Print," *The Advocate,* June 30, 1992.
4. Leigh W. Rutledge, *The Gay Fireside Companion,* Boston: Alyson, 1989.
5. "Dossier," *The Advocate,* April 7, 1992.
6. *Alternatives: Gays and Lesbians in the Newsroom,* American Society of Newspaper Editors Human Resources Committee Report, April 1990.
7. Overlooked Opinions, Inc., Chicago, 1993.
8. InfoTrac, Information Access Company, Foster City, Calif., 1993.
9. "Dossier," *The Advocate,* April 23, 1991.
10. Steve Greenberg, "Amanda Bearse: Married . . . with a Child," *The Advocate,* September 21, 1993.
11. Mimi=Freed, "Are They Laughing Out There?" *The Advocate,* December 14, 1993.
12. *Sex & Sexuality Index,* Journal Graphics, Denver, 1993.
13. "This Way Out," Los Angeles, 1993.
14. Michael Kuchwara, "Twenty-Five Years after 'The Boys in the Band,'" Associated Press, October 24, 1993.
15. Ken Furtado and Nancy Hellner, eds., *Gay and Lesbian American Plays: An Annotated Bibliography,* Metuchen, New Jersey: Scarecrow, 1993.
16. Steve Stewart, *Gay Hollywood Film and Video Guide,* Laguna Hills, Calif.: Companion, 1993.
17. Frameline, San Francisco, 1993.
18. Rick Harding, "FCC Says It Received 13 Formal Complaints about 'Tongues Untied,'" *The Advocate,* September 10, 1991.
19. "Year in Review," *The Advocate,* July 2, 1991.
20. *Hostile Climate: A State by State Report on Anti-gay Activities,* New York: People for the American Way, 1993.
21. Bob Summer, "A Niche Market Comes of Age," *Publishers Weekly,* June 29, 1992.
22. Gay and Lesbian Task Force of the American Library Association, 1993.
23. Eric Bryant, "Where Do You Shelve Books That Are Out of the Closet?," *Publishers Weekly,* June 7, 1993.
24. Bob Summer, "Gay and Lesbian Publishing: The Paradox of Success," *Publishers Weekly,* June 7, 1993.
25. Victoria A. Brownworth, "Black Out," *The Advocate,* August 13, 1992.

"There are no known homosexuals in the corps of cadets or regular Army. None!"

Colonel John P. Yeagley, United States Military Academy
public affairs officer, to reporters, 1986

Supplanted by prejudice, facts were notoriously absent from the recent debate over the suitability of gay men and lesbians for military service. Pentagon reports and independent surveys, long suppressed, reveal that even the military's own analysts have concluded that lesbians and gay men have served in the U.S. military honorably and that their presence has resulted in no damage to unit cohesiveness, morale, or security. Further, General Accounting Office estimates show that the ban costs American taxpayers millions of dollars per year. Exact costs are impossible to determine, however, because the figures on discharges for homosexuality do not account for service personnel, homosexual and heterosexual, who resign voluntarily or whose official discharge does not mention homosexuality.

Lieutenant Gotthold Frederick Enslin, discharged on March 11, 1778, is the first known solider to be dismissed from the U.S. military for homosexuality. [1]

Punishment of homosexual soldiers was first codified in U.S. military law during World War I. [1]

The first attempt to purge homosexuals occurred in 1919 at the Naval Training Station in Newport, Rhode Island. [1]

The prohibition on gay men and lesbians in the military was instituted in 1943. Since then, nearly 100,000 men and women have been discharged from the military for alleged homosexuality. [2]

By some counts, up to 80% of all women who served in World War II were lesbians. [1]

Military lesbians estimated that lesbians constituted up to 35% of women in uniform during the early 1980s. [1]

During World War II, the military examined nearly 18,000,000 men and rejected only 4,000 to 5,000 as homosexual. [2]

The Crittenden committee's 639-page report, written in 1957, concluded that there "was no sound basis" to assume that homosexuals pose a security risk. The report further stated that "there have been many known instances of individuals who have served honorably and well, despite being exclusively homosexual." For nearly 20 years, the Pentagon denied that this report existed. [1]

During the past decade, gay people have served as generals in every branch of the armed forces. [1]

Between 1980 and 1990, white women accounted for 6% of all personnel serving in the U.S. armed forces and for 20% of all discharged for homosexuality. [3]

In the Marine Corps during this period, women represented 5% of all personnel and 28% of all discharges for homosexuality. [3]

Between 1980 and 1990, 16,919 men and women were discharged for homosexuality. Most of these were enlisted (99%), white (83%), and male (77%). [3]

The total number of discharges for homosexuality dropped 47% between 1980 and 1990. [3]

Between 1986 and 1990, the Department of Defense conducted 3,663 investigations of alleged cases of homosexuality. 5,951 personnel were discharged for homosexuality during this period. [1,3]

Locking suspected gays in closets became a popular military interrogation technique during the 1980s. [1]

Gay discharges increased during the Carter administration. [1]

There were more discharges for homosexuality in 1980 than at any time since the McCarthy era. [1]

The cost of replacing the 932 military personnel discharged for homosexuality in 1990 was approximately $27 million. [3]

Since 1982, almost 95% of military personnel discharged for homosexuality have received an honorable or general discharge. [3]

Of the 16 members of North Atlantic Treaty Organization, only the United States and Britain exclude gay men and lesbians from military service. [4]

A study of the Royal Netherlands Navy—possibly the only study of a country that has lifted its prohibition on gay military service—revealed that verbal abuse of gays and lesbians in the armed forces remains widespread two decades after that country's ban was lifted. Lesbians reported fewer service-related difficulties than gay men. [5]

In Canada, where the ban on lesbians and gay men in the military was struck down by court order in 1992, there were no reports of lowered morale or impaired unit cohesiveness within the armed forces. [6]

Two federal appeals courts have ruled that the military ban on gay men and lesbians is unconstitutional: a panel of the Ninth Circuit in California in a 1988 ruling in the case of Perry Watkins and a panel of the U.S. Court of Appeals for the District of Columbia in a 1993 ruling in the case of Joseph Steffan. [7]

At least 14 openly gay or lesbian service members were dispatched to the Persian Gulf War. [8]

During the 11 days after President Clinton's inauguration, the subject of gay men and lesbians in the U.S. military appeared on the front page of the *New York Times* 9 times. [9]

Of the 17 witnesses called to testify on the first day of Senate hearings on Clinton's proposal to lift the ban on gay military service, only 2 spoke in favor of lifting the ban. As they spoke, roughly one-fifth of the uniformed personnel in the hearing room walked out. [10]

SOURCES

1. Randy Shilts, *Conduct Unbecoming,* New York: St. Martin's, 1993.
2. Allan Bérubé, *Coming Out Under Fire: The History of Gay Men and Women in World War Two,* New York: Plume, 1990.

3. General Accounting Office, "DOD's Policy on Homosexuality," June 1992.

4. "In NATO, Only U.S. and Britain Ban Gay Soldiers," *New York Times,* November 13, 1992.

5. "Lifting the Ban Doesn't Open the Closets," *San Francisco Weekly,* December 16, 1992.

6. "Little Trouble in Canada When Its Gay Ban Ended," *New York Times,* January 31, 1993.

7. Stephen Labaton, "Military Rebuffed by Appeals Court over Homosexuality," *New York Times,* November 17, 1993.

8. John Zeh, "War May Bring Changes to Military's Gay Policy," *San Francisco Sentinel,* March 14, 1991.

9. *New York Times,* January 21–January 31, 1993.

10. "Panel Told That Lifting the Ban Would Cost Lives," *San Francisco Chronicle,* May 11, 1993.

"Although there is now a consensus that gays, like other minorities, deserve protection from job discrimination, they are still viewed as being outside of the mainstream. . . . In fact, despite a 15-percentage point increase since 1982 in public support for giving gays equal protection on the job (from 59% to 74%), over the same period acceptance of homosexuality as a life-style has increased only marginally (from 34% to 38%)."

Gallup Poll, 1992

With growing numbers of voters across the country facing ballot measures that would deny rights to gay men and lesbians, public opinion on sexual orientation issues is a critical arena. We wonder, however, if it is perhaps time to ask some new questions. For example, nearly half of Americans say they believe being gay or lesbian is a choice—but how many believe that being *heterosexual* is a choice? Furthermore, 44% of U.S. residents say that same-sex sexual relations should remain criminalized—but how many would say that the government has a right to regulate the activity of consenting adults in private? Answers to these questions notwithstanding, it is clear that visibility plays a key role in shaping opinions on gay and lesbian issues: people who actually know someone who is gay or lesbian tend to be far more supportive of gay and lesbian rights than those who do not.

In a national poll conducted in 1965, 82% of men and 58% of women said that homosexuality represents a "clear threat" to the American way of life. [1]

In 1993, 46% of Americans said homosexuality is "a chosen lifestyle"; 32% said being gay or lesbian is innate. [2]

35% of those surveyed in a 1985 *Los Angeles Times* poll said they feel uncomfortable around gay men and lesbians. [3]

In a 1988 study of junior and senior high school students, 12% of respondents said it would be "good" or "very good" to have a lesbian or gay person move into their neighborhood, while 37% thought it would be "acceptable." Between 50% and 60% of respondents said it would be "good" or "very good" to have neighbors of different racial or ethnic backgrounds, and approximately 90% thought having such neighbors was acceptable. [4]

In a 1989 survey of San Francisco residents, 49% said there are "too many" or "somewhat too many" gay people living in San Francisco. [1]

51% of first-year college students surveyed in 1991 said they think lesbians and gay men should try to be heterosexual. [5]

In the same survey, 22% of the students reported that they had verbally harassed gay men; 8% described themselves as "approving" or "very approving" of homosexuality, while 54% described themselves as "disapproving" or "very disapproving" of homosexuality. [5]

In 1977, 56% of Americans said homosexuals should have equal rights in employment. That number rose to 74% in 1992. [1, 6]

11% of Americans would object to having a gay airline pilot. [7]

55% of Americans would object to having a gay elementary school teacher. [7]

49% of Americans would object to having a gay doctor. [7]

In a 1993 *U.S. News and World Report* poll of 1,000 registered voters, 53% said they personally knew someone who is gay; of these, 73% supported equal rights for lesbians and gay men. 46% said they do not know someone who is lesbian or gay; of these, 55% supported equal rights for lesbians and gay men. [2]

In 1977, 43% of Americans said it should be illegal for consenting adults to engage in homosexual relations. The number rose to 54% in 1991 and fell to 44% in 1992. [1, 6]

In 1982, 66% of Americans said they believe homosexuals are likely to lead less happy, well adjusted lives than heterosexuals. [1]

When asked whether sexual relations between two adults of the same sex were *always* wrong, the following percentages of the United States population said yes: [8]

	1973	1980	1985	1989
General population (%)	73	73	75	74
Males (%)	72	73	75	75
Females (%)	74	74	75	73
Whites (%)	71	73	74	73
Blacks (%)	83	79	84	80
Other races (%)	69	44	79	82
18–23 years old (%)	55	66	70	75
30–35 years old (%)	75	61	67	71
36–41 years old (%)	76	72	65	63
66+ years old (%)	91	88	92	86

In 1993, 66.3% of the American population believed that sexual relations between two consenting adults of the same sex were always wrong. [8]

SOURCES

1. Leigh W. Rutledge, *The Gay Fireside Companion,* Boston: Alyson, 1989.
2. *U.S. News & World Report,* July 5, 1993.
3. John C. Gonsiorek and James D. Weinrich, eds., *Homosexuality: Research Implications for Public Policy,* Newbury Park, Calif.: Sage, 1991.
4. Gregory M. Herek and Kevin T. Berrill, eds., *Hate Crimes: Confronting Violence against Lesbians and Gay Men,* Newbury Park, Calif.: Sage, 1992.
5. Gary David Comstock, *Violence against Lesbians and Gay Men,* New York: Columbia University Press, 1991.
6. *The Gallup Poll: Public Opinion 1992,* Wilmington, Del.: Scholarly Resources Inc., 1993.
7. Jeffrey Schmalz, "Poll Finds an Even Split on Homosexuality's Cause," *New York Times,* March 5, 1993.
8. National Opinion Research Center at the University of Chicago, Chicago, 1973–93.

"Joining a religious community from about 500 [A.D.] to about 1300 [A.D.] was probably the surest way of meeting other gay people [in Europe]."

John Boswell, "Homosexuality and Religious Life:
A Historical Approach," 1989

Although religion has been a major source of oppression for sexual minorities, increasing numbers of gay men and lesbians are asserting their place within religious institutions. The Metropolitan Community Church, a Christian church whose primary outreach is to the gay and lesbian community, is flourishing worldwide, while gay men and lesbians continue their fight to gain full acceptance within other established religious bodies. And while the religious right continues to use the Bible as evidence of the immorality of homosexuality, gay and lesbian religion scholars have shown that what many perceive as irrefutable condemnation of homosexuality within the Bible is in fact a matter of interpretation and translation.

Among world religions, Buddhism is notable in that it does not condemn homosexuality. [1]

Islam, with more than 6 million adherents in the United States, is the world's fastest growing religion. Although the Koran does not condemn homosexuality per se, Islamic law punishes men and women found guilty of "public" homosexual behavior that is witnessed by four adult males. [2,3]

There are approximately 1 billion adherents of Christianity in the world and 142 million in the United States, including 79 million Protestants and 52 million Roman Catholics—equivalent to 60% of the United States population. In 1983, roughly 22% of the U.S. population ages 18 and older were Evangelical Christians, according to a public opinion survey. Of these, 88.7% expressed strong opposition to homosexuality. [1,4]

Pat Robertson's Christian Coalition has 250,000 members in 49 states, controls the Republican committees in 6 states, and had some 300 delegates at the 1992 Republican National Convention, including more than a quarter of the platform committee. Opposing homosexuality and restricting gay and lesbian rights are among the Coalition's primary objectives. [5]

A conservative estimate of the percentage of homosexual men and women in the Catholic priesthood and religious life is around 30%, with approximately the same number in the Protestant ministry and the rabbinate. [6]

Of readers of *Out/Look* (a gay and lesbian magazine) surveyed in 1991, 83% were raised in the Christian tradition and 11% were raised in the Jewish tradition; 58% said spirituality was very important to them, while 28% said religion was very important to them. [7]

The word "homosexual" did not appear in any translation of the Christian Bible until 1946. [2]

There are words in Greek for same-sex sexual activities, yet they never appear in the original text of the New Testament. [2]

The Bible says nothing about homosexuality per se as a sexual orientation but refers only to certain kinds of acts, primarily homosexual temple prostitution. [2]

Depending on which version is cited and how the Hebrew and Greek words are translated, 8 references to homosexuality are commonly cited in Judeo-Christian scripture: Genesis 19; Leviticus 18:22, 20:13; Romans 1:18–32; I Corinthians 6:9; I Timothy 1:10, and Revelations 21:8, 22:15. [8]

Of the 47 religious bodies examined in Dr. J. Gordon Melton's *The Churches Speak on: Homosexuality, 1991:*
- 8 have released statements supporting lesbian and gay rights
- 4 have stated that homosexuality and traditional Christian moral precepts are compatible
- 9 have distinguished between homosexual behavior, which they consider a sin, and homosexuality as an orientation
- 3 will ordain "out" lesbians and gays
- 4 will perform some sort of commitment ceremony for same-sex couples
- 34 condemn homosexuals and homosexuality as an abomination. [9]

The beginning of an open dialogue between Christian leaders and the homosexual community can be traced to the formation of the Council on Religion and the Homosexual in San Francisco in 1964. [9]

In 1969 the Church of Christ's Council on Christian Social Action adopted one of the first position statements on homosexuality, in which it called for the decriminalization of homosexual activities between consenting adults. [9]

In 1972 the United Church of Christ became the first Christian denomination to ordain an openly gay candidate. [10]

The first openly lesbian priest in a major Christian denomination, Ellen Marie Barrett, was ordained by the Episcopal Church in January 1977. [11]

The first lesbian or gay union performed by a major religious body occurred in 1984, within the Unitarian Universalist Church. [11]

From the fifth century on, gay clerics apparently took part in homosexual marriage ceremonies, which were widely known in the Catholic world. [12]

In a 1989 survey of 101 gay Catholic priests:
- Two-thirds of the sample estimated that 40%–60% of the Catholic clergy are gay
- 63% reported "leading a celibate life" as a frequent source of problems
- 36.6% occasionally had been sexually active with another person
- 36.6% frequently had been sexually active with another person
- 82.2% said they would "probably" or "definitely" stay in the priesthood. [13]

According to the *Encyclopedia of Homosexuality*, there is evidence that at least 10 popes were gay or bisexual. [1]

GAY AND LESBIAN RELIGIOUS INSTITUTIONS
The first gay church was Charles Webster Leadbeater's Anglican-derived Liberal Catholic Church, founded in Sydney, Australia, in 1916. [14]

The first American church organized primarily for homosexuals is thought to have been the one formed in Atlanta in 1946 by George Hyde, a youth minister in the independent Catholic Movement. [9]

The United Fellowship of Metropolitan Community Churches (MCC)—a Christian church whose primary outreach is to lesbians and gay men—was founded in 1968 by the Reverend Troy Perry. [15]

There are currently 23,561 Roman Catholic churches, 200 Scientology churches, and 230 MCC churches in the United States. Worldwide, MCC now has more than 32,000 members and 291 churches in 17 countries. [15]

The world's largest lesbian and gay congregation is the Cathedral of Hope Metropolitan Community Church in Dallas, with 892 active members and 2,100 constituent members. Average attendance is 750 per week. [11]

The MCC's total income in 1992 exceeded $10 million, making it the largest nonprofit organization serving lesbians and gay men. [15]

18 MCC churches experienced arson between 1971 and 1985. [15]

One of the largest gay and lesbian Jewish congregations in the United States is Beth Simchat Torah in New York City, with about 1,000 members. [16]

Dignity, an organization of gay Catholics working within the Roman Catholic Church, has 6,000 dues-paying members. [11]

From 1986 to1991, 50 chapters of Dignity were expelled from Roman Catholic church property. [17]

SOURCES

1. Wayne R. Dynes, ed., *Encyclopedia of Homosexuality*, New York: Garland, 1990.
2. Warren J. Blumenfeld and Diane Raymond, *Looking at Gay and Lesbian Life*, Boston: Beacon, 1988.
3. *Alyson Almanac 1994–95 Edition*, Boston: Alyson, 1993.
4. James Davison Hunter, *American Evangelicalism*, Rutgers: Rutgers University, 1983.
5. "Rise of the Religious Right," *The New Leader*, September 21, 1992.
6. *The Catholic Church, Homosexuality and Social Justice: The Report by the Task Force on Gay and Lesbian Issues*, Commission on Social Justice, Archdiocese of San Francisco, 1982.
7. Reader's Survey, *Out/Look*, Fall 1991.
8. Gary David Comstock, *Violence against Lesbians and Gay Men*, New York: Columbia University Press, 1991.
9. J. Gordon Melton, *The Churches Speak on: Homosexuality*, Detroit: Gale Research, 1991.

10. Robert Nugent and Jeannine Gramick, "Homosexuality: Protestant, Catholic, and Jewish Issues, a Fishbone Tail" in Richard Hasbany, ed., *Homosexuality and Religion,* Binghamton, N.Y.: Harrington Park, 1989.

11. Lynne Yamaguchi Fletcher, *The First Gay Pope and Other Records,* Boston: Alyson, 1992.

12. John Boswell, "Homosexuality and Religious Life: A Historical Approach" in *Homosexuality, the Priesthood and the Religious Life,* edited by Jeannine Gramick, New York: Crossroad, 1989.

13. James G. Wolf, *Gay Priests,* New York: Harper & Row, 1989.

14. Wayne R. Dynes and Stephen Donaldson, eds., *Homosexuality and Religion and Philosophy,* New York: Garland, 1992.

15. "The Universal Fellowship of Metropolitan Community Churches Fact Sheet," Universal Fellowship of Metropolitan Community Churches, 1993.

16. Chris Bull, "Conservative Jews Face Growing Rift over Gay Issues," *The Advocate,* May 5, 1992.

17. Rick Harding, "Minneapolis Panel: Catholic Officials Violated Bias Law," *The Advocate,* January 1, 1991.

"For gay liberation, there was no 'normal' or 'perverse' sexuality, only a world of sexual possibilities ranged against a repressive order of marriage, oedipal families, and compulsory heterosexuality."

Barry D. Adam, *The Rise of a Gay and Lesbian Movement,* 1987

According to the World Health Organization, 100 million acts of sexual intercourse occur every day. For gay men, sexual practices have shifted dramatically since the advent of AIDS. Part of this "sexual revolution" involves increased use of adult videos and magazines as an alternative to unsafe sex; however, current figures on the amount of pornography produced or consumed by the gay and lesbian community are unavailable. Indeed, while there is no shortage of information on heterosexual pornography, gay—and especially lesbian—pornography is vastly underdocumented. And though it is clear that the gay sex industry has provided extensive financial support to the gay community and, through advertising revenue, to gay publications, it is difficult to document how gay men and lesbians feel about the role that the sex industry plays in gay and lesbian life.

In a 1983 study of American couples who had been together two years or less:
- 33% of the lesbian couples had sex three times a week or more
- 67% of the gay male couples had sex three times a week or more
- 45% of the married couples had sex three times a week or more
- 61% of the cohabiting heterosexual couples had sex three times a week or more
- Lesbian couples reported being most satisfied with their sexual relationships. [1]

Of couples who had been together between two and ten years:
- 7% of the lesbian couples had sex three times a week or more
- 32% of the gay male couples had sex three times a week or more
- 27% of the married couples had sex three times a week or more
- 38% of the cohabiting heterosexual couples had sex three times a week or more
- Lesbian couples reported being most satisfied with their sexual relationships. [1]

In the same study, 95% of lesbians, 71% of gay men, and 80% of heterosexuals reported kissing every time they had sex. 12% of lesbians, 17% of gay men, and 6% of heterosexuals also reported having oral sex every time they had sex. [1]

In a 1987 study, 71% of gay men and 44% of lesbians claimed they could look at someone they did not know and identify that person's sexual orientation. Only 20% of the total sample exceeded chance levels of correct detection. [2]

In a 1991 analysis of the brains of 41 cadavers (19 of them gay, all of them male), Dr. Simon LeVay found that the hypothalamus—an area of the brain believed to control sexual activity—was less than half the size in the gay men than in the heterosexual men. [3]

The magazine *Sexology* concludes that gay men have larger penises than heterosexual men: an average of 3.3 inches in length and 1.08 inches in width (when limp) versus 3 inches in length and 1 inch in width. [4]

The average American male will have approximately 6,500 orgasms during his lifetime. [5]

During fiscal year 1991–1992, Gay Men's Health Crisis in New York City distributed 1,500,000 condoms. [6]

SEX INDUSTRY

According to the 1993 edition of *Bob Damron's Address Book,* there are 1,216 "cruisy areas" for gay men in the United States and 39 "adult" theaters exclusively for gay men in the United States. [7]

The same guide lists 430 "adult" book/video stores, many with peep-show video booths, that cater to gay men in the United States. According to the Meese Commission's 1986 report on pornography, it has been estimated that peep shows are the most lucrative segment of the pornography industry, with annual net profits projected at two billion dollars. [7, 8]

In 1988 there were 1,250 "adult" videos released, earning $360 million and 20.5% of the revenue in the stores that stock them. [9]

Since the mid-1980's, approximately 20 lesbian-produced sex videos have been released. During the same period an additional 500 videos featuring women having sex with women were created mainly for a straight male audience. [10]

Fatale Video, the largest and oldest lesbian video company, distributes 10 films, each selling between 1,200 and 1,500 copies a year. [10]

Bijou Video, a video distributor, lists 2,720 gay male videos in its 1993 catalog. [11]

50% of all gay newspapers rely on phone-sex ads for advertising sales. [12]

The Club Baths chain was founded in Cleveland in 1965. At its peak there were 42 franchises. 5 are still operating, and there are now 10 Club Body Centers throughout the United States. [13]

According to *Bob Damron's Address Book* for 1993, there are 67 "spa/saunas" (open twenty-four hours a day) in the United States. [7]

In a survey of 807 men leaving "spa/saunas" in Los Angeles County:
- 72.4% went to the establishment to have sex
- 61% reported behaviors associated with low risk of HIV transmission
- 10% reported high-risk behavior
- 97% reported familiarity with information on AIDS distributed in the bathhouse. [14]

In a 1989 study of male sex workers, 70% of whom were gay or bisexual and 30% of whom were heterosexual:
- The average age of first sex act for money was 15.9 years
- Money was the main motive for work
- Average income was $50 per customer; average salary was $561.89 per week
- 86% have sex other than for money regularly
- 83.7% had been arrested by the police (48% for prostitution)
- 78% used drugs on a regular basis
- 96% were aware of AIDS

- 58% had changed sexual practices because of AIDS
- 42% had had some form of sexually transmitted disease
- 40.9% had required hospitalization as a result of physical violence from clients. [15]

SEX IN PRISON

Available surveys find that 17%–69% of prison inmates, male and female, report a homosexual experience while in prison. [16]

A 1982 random sampling of the male prison population in a California state institution housing 2,500 inmates found:
- 65% of inmates reported having sex while in prison
- 20.5% reported performing oral sex
- 51.5% reported receiving sex orally
- 38.5% reported performing anal sex
- 20.5% reported having been anally penetrated. [17]

In the same study, a sampling of male inmates who identified themselves as gay revealed:
- 1.3% would rather be straight
- 52.5% reported frequently being pressured sexually by other inmates
- 88.8% reported that most of their sexual partners considered themselves to be straight. [17]

SOURCES

1. Phillip Blumstein and Pepper Schwartz, *American Couples,* New York: Morrow, 1983.
2. Gregory Berger et al., "Detection of Sexual Orientation by Heterosexuals and Homosexuals," *Journal of Homosexuality* 13 (no. 4), 1987.
3. David Gelman et al., "Born or Bred?" *Newsweek,* February 24, 1992.
4. Leigh W. Rutledge, *The Gay Decades: From Stonewall to the Present, the People and Events That Shaped Gay Lives,* New York: Plume, 1992.
5. Leigh W. Rutledge, *The Gay Fireside Companion,* Boston: Alyson, 1989.
6. "Gay Men's Health Crisis Fact Sheet," New York, 1993.
7. *The 29th Edition of Bob Damron's Address Book,* San Francisco: Damron, 1993.
8. Gordon Hawkins and Franklin E. Zimring, *Pornography in a Free Society,* New York: Cambridge University Press, 1988.
9. "Porn No Flesh in the Pan; Back on the Rise after Having Cleaned Up Its Act," *Variety,* January 17, 1990.
10. Roxxie, "Girls on Film," *The Advocate,* October 20, 1992.
11. *Bijou Video Catalog,* Chicago, 1993.

12. Jonathan Curiel, "Gay Newspapers," *Editor and Publisher,* August 3, 1991.

13. Andrew Holleran, "Steam, Soap, and Sex," *The Advocate,* October 6, 1992.

14. Gary A. Richwald et al., "Sexual Activity in Bathhouses in Los Angeles County: Implications for AIDS Prevention and Education," *Journal of Sex Research* 25, May 1988.

15. C. M. Earls et al.,"Male Prostitution," *Archives of Sexual Behavior* 18, October 1989.

16. Alice M. Propper, *Prison Homosexuality: Myth and Reality,* Lexington, Mass.: Lexington, 1981.

17. Wayne S. Wooden and Jay Parker, *Men Behind Bars: Sexual Exploitation in Prison,* New York: Plenum, 1982.

"I put prostitutes and queers at the same level . . . and I'd be hard-put to give somebody life for killing a prostitute."

Dallas judge Jack Hampton, 1989

It is sobering to discover how many organizations and resources are devoted to defending gay men and lesbians against homophobic violence. Equally disquieting is the fact that most antigay and antilesbian violence is committed by young males under 21. What drives young men to attack lesbians and gay men? Tacit approval of gay bashing comes from certain members of the judicial system, from the print and visual media, and from antigay lyrics, such as the 1992 reggae hit "Boom Bye Bye," in which Buju Banton encourages listeners to shoot gay men: "Faggots have to run, or get a bullet in the head. Bang-bang in a faggot's head. . . . Two men necking, lying in a bed. Hugging each other, and caressing one another's legs. Get an automatic or an Uzi instead." The impact of such explicitly antigay sentiments has not been directly studied, but it is undoubtedly a factor in the alarming rise of violence directed against the lesbian and gay community.

According to the U.S. Department of Justice, the most frequent victims of hate violence today are African Americans, Latinos, Southeast Asians, Jews, and lesbians and gay men. "Homosexuals are probably the most frequent victims." [1]

Of 4,558 bias-related crimes reported to the FBI in 1992, 422 were described as antilesbian or antigay. By contrast, the National Gay and Lesbian Task Force logged 1,001 hate crimes against lesbians and gay men in just five cities—Boston, Chicago, Minneapolis and St. Paul, New York, and San Francisco—for the same time period. [2]

20 states, the District of Columbia, and 11 cities and counties have enacted hate-crime legislation that includes crimes based on sexual orientation. [2]

In Colorado, reports of antilesbian and antigay violence tripled in November and December of 1992 after voters approved Amendment Two, prohibiting enactment of laws that protect lesbians and gay men from discrimination. [2]

More than half of all socially active lesbians and gay men have experienced some sort of antilesbian and antigay violence. Such incidents are most likely to occur in a public lesbian or gay space, such as a bar or community center. [3]

The first national survey focusing exclusively on violence against lesbians and gay men was conducted by the National Gay and Lesbian Task Force in 1984. Of survey respondents:
- 94% had experienced some type of victimization
- 19% had been punched, kicked, hit, or beaten at least once because of their sexual orientation
- 44% had been threatened with physical violence because of their sexual orientation. [4]

In a summary of 26 antilesbian and antigay violence or victimization surveys conducted between 1977 and 1991:
- 80% of respondents were verbally harassed
- 44% were threatened with violence
- 33% were chased or followed
- 25% were pelted with objects
- 19% experienced vandalism
- 17% were physically assaulted
- 13% were spat on
- 9% were assaulted with an object or weapon. [4]

There are no community-based data-collection systems that measure antilesbian and antigay violence at the national level. [2]

In the five major U.S. cities that have professionally staffed agencies that monitor antilesbian and antigay violence—Boston, Chicago, Minneapolis and St. Paul, New York, and San Francisco—reports of antigay and antilesbian incidents increased by 172% between 1988 and 1992:
- In 1988, 697 incidents were reported
- In 1989, 949 incidents were reported
- In 1990, 1,389 incidents were reported
- In 1991, 1,822 incidents were reported
- In 1992, 1,898 incidents were reported. [2]

Antigay or antilesbian homicides climbed 50%, from 8 in 1991 to 12 in 1992. [4]

The Klanwatch Project of the Southern Poverty Law Center documented 31 bias-motivated murders in 1992. [2]

In 1992, for the third year in a row, New York City led the nation in antilesbian and antigay violence, with 662 reported incidents. San Francisco ranked second, with 435 reported incidents. [5]

Of the 662 antilesbian and antigay incidents reported in New York City in 1992, victims were physically assaulted in 49% of the incidents against individuals. [5]

Of the 479 crimes recorded by the bias unit of the New York City police in 1992, 86 were classified as antigay or antilesbian. Of the three homicides reported by the New York Gay and Lesbian Anti-Violence Project in 1992 none was classified as a bias crime by the unit. [5]

Of the 500 lesbian, gay, and bisexual youths who used the services of the Hetrick-Martin Institute of New York City in 1988, 40% had experienced violent attacks. [4]

In studies of lesbian and gay victimization on four college campuses—Oberlin College (1990), Rutgers University (1987), Pennsylvania State University (1989), and Yale University (1986)—16%–26% of respondents had been threatened with physical violence, and 3%–5% reported that they had been the target of physical assaults. [2]

The most common perpetrators of antilesbian and antigay violence—responsible for 50% of all reported incidents—are youths ages 21 or under; 94% of the perpetrators are male. About two-thirds of the perpetrators are unknown to the victims. [3]

Acquaintances and policemen are, respectively, the second and third most common perpetrators of antilesbian and antigay violence. [3]

Surveys measuring antigay abuse by relatives found that between 16% and 41% of respondents have experienced verbal insults or intimidation by relatives, and 4%–8% reported physical violence. [4]

72% of white victims of antigay and antilesbian violence did not report incidents to the police, according to surveys, while 82% of gay and lesbian people of color did not report such incidents. The main reason appears to be the perception that the police are antigay. [3, 4]

As of 1992, only 2 studies on antilesbian and antigay victimization and violence had examined racial and ethnic differences in rates of victimization. Both found that lesbians and gay men of color are at greater risk for violent attack because of their sexual orientation. [4]

In an overview of 26 studies of antilesbian and antigay harassment and violence, 20% of lesbians and gay men reported some form of victimization by police. [4]

89% of all incidents reported to the New York City Anti-Violence Project in 1992 resulted in no arrest. [5]

In a review of National Gay and Lesbian Task Force surveys of antilesbian and antigay violence and victimization between 1986 and 1989, between 14% and 17% of the incidents documented were AIDS related. [2]

SOURCES

1. National Institute of Justice, U.S. Department of Justice, "The Response of the Criminal Justice System to Bias Crime: An Exploratory Review," 1987.
2. National Gay and Lesbian Task Force Policy Institute, *Anti-Gay/Lesbian Violence, Victimization and Defamation in 1992,* Washington, D.C., 1993.
3. Gary David Comstock, *Violence against Lesbians and Gay Men,* New York: Columbia University Press, 1991.
4. Gregory M. Herek and Kevin T. Berrill, eds., *Hate Crimes: Confronting Violence against Lesbians and Gay Men,* Newbury Park, Calif.: Sage, 1992.
5. *1992 Annual Report,* New York City Gay and Lesbian Anti-Violence Project, 1993.

"The workplace, in which we spend more than half our waking lives, is rapidly emerging as the frontier of lesbian and gay activism."

James D. Woods, *The Corporate Closet,* 1993

Although the nation's largest employer, the armed forces, continues to insist that gay men and lesbians are unfit to serve in its ranks, other public employers have begun to recruit gay men and lesbians. At the same time, scores of private companies have taken steps to provide benefits to the domestic partners of gay men and lesbians. Despite these strides, however, it appears that the vast majority of lesbian and gay employees remain in the closet at work, acutely conscious of the stigmatization that often accompanies coming out in the workplace.

The three most common job categories for gay men are management, health care, and education. [1]

40% more gay men and lesbians are employed in finance and insurance than in the arts. [2]

Ten times as many gay men and lesbians work with computers as work in the fashion industry. [2]

In a 1991 survey, *Partners* magazine found that 8% of lesbians and gay men had employers who provide same-sex partners with some employee benefits. [3]

The following labor unions are on record as supporting lesbian and gay civil rights:
- American Federation of Labor / Congress of Industrial Organizations
- American Federation of State, County and Municipal Employees
- American Federation of Teachers
- National Education Association. [4]

PUBLIC EMPLOYMENT
In 1953, President Dwight D. Eisenhower signed Executive Order 10450, mandating that "sexual perverts" be fired from federal jobs. As a result,

an average of 40 homosexuals per month were removed from government posts between April 1953 and July 1954. [5]

During the McCarthy era, more people lost their jobs for being alleged homosexuals than for being Communists. [5]

In 1976, the Carter administration issued a new standard for federal employment, stating that the private lives of federal employees were not relevant to federal personnel decisions. [6]

In October 1993, 3 congressmen from Oklahoma declared that they would not hire an openly gay or lesbian person for their staffs. [7]

As of January 1993, 130 municipalities prohibit employment discrimination on the basis of sexual orientation. [8]

Until 1993, the Dallas Police Department refused to hire lesbians or gays because the state's sodomy law criminalized same-sex conduct. [9]

As of 1992, police departments in ten U.S. cities had made attempts to recruit gays: Atlanta; Boston; Los Angeles; Madison, Wisconsin; Minneapolis; New York City; Philadelphia; Portland, Oregon; San Francisco; and Seattle. [9]

Current estimates of gay police officers within the New York City Police Department population range from 10% to upward of 30%. [9]

As of August 1991, there were no publicly gay police officers in Chicago's 12,000-member police force. [9]

PRIVATE EMPLOYMENT

Whether official or unofficial, there is a gay and lesbian employees' organization in every large company in the United States. [2]

More than 100 major companies have stated that they do not discriminate on the basis of sexual orientation. [4]

In a 1987 *Wall Street Journal* survey, 66% of major-company chief executive officers said they would be reluctant to put a homosexual on management committees. [2]

In 1993, the National Gay and Lesbian Task Force sent surveys to the 1,000 largest companies in the country; 757 companies failed to reply; 145 companies refused to comply. Of the 98 companies that did return the survey, 5 offer domestic-partner benefits to same-sex partners, half include sexual orientation issues in diversity training, and more than two-thirds offer some type of support for people with HIV. [10]

Two-thirds of gay employees have witnessed some sort of hostility toward gay people on the job.[2]

1 in 4 respondents in a 1987 national poll said they would "strongly object" to working around gay men and lesbians; 27% said they "would prefer not to do so." [6]

The Cracker Barrel Old Country Stores, a restaurant chain based in Tennessee, fired at least nine gay and lesbian employees in 1991 because their "sexual preferences fail[ed] to demonstrate normal heterosexual values." [11]

Of 191 employers surveyed in Anchorage, Alaska, in 1987–1988:
- 18% said they would fire a known homosexual
- 27% said they would not hire a known homosexual
- 26% said they would not promote a known homosexual. [8]

The largest award ever made to an individual for a gay-employment-bias claim was $5.3 million to Dr. Jeffrey Collins, a California resident who was fired after his secretary found a memo in the office photocopier detailing rules for a safe-sex party. (The award was subsequently reduced on appeal.) [8]

In February 1992, Levi-Strauss & Co., with 23,000 workers, became the largest U.S. employer to offer health insurance to partners of lesbians and gay men. [8]

COMING OUT AT WORK
In a summary of 12 discrimination studies conducted from 1980 to 1991, an average of 58% of the lesbians and gay men surveyed feared discrimination or concealed their sexual orientation at work. [4]

62% of lesbians and gay men surveyed in 1992 by *Out/Look* said a major incentive for coming out at work was to avoid difficulties created by pretending to be straight. [8]

62% of *Out/Look* readers said that their sexual orientation "always" or "often" is a source of stress at work, and 46% said it influenced their choice of careers. [8]

In the same *Out/Look* survey:
- 93% had "come out" to at least one co-worker
- 68% had discussed a same-sex lover with someone at work
- 30% had displayed a photo, ring, or some other symbol of a relationship at work
- 74% had been vocal on gay political issues. [8]

SOURCES

1. Overlooked Opinions, Inc., Chicago, Ill., 1993.
2. Mark D. Fefer, "Gay in Corporate America," *Fortune,* December 16, 1991.
3. *Partners,* Partners Task Force for Gay and Lesbian Couples, May/June, 1991.
4. National Gay and Lesbian Task Force, Washington, D.C., 1993.
5. John D'Emilio, *Sexual Politics, Sexual Communities: The Making of a Homosexual Minority in the United States, 1940–1970,* Chicago: University of Chicago Press, 1983.
6. John C. Gonsiorek and James D. Weinrich, eds., *Homosexuality: Research Implications for Public Policy,* Newbury Park, Calif.: Sage, 1991.
7. Kevin Merida and Kenneth J. Cooper, "3 Congressmen Won't Hire Gays; Speaker Sort of Denounces Them," *Washington Post,* October 22, 1993.
8. James D. Woods with Jay H. Lucas, *The Corporate Closet: The Professional Lives of Gay Men in America,* New York: Free Press, 1993.
9. Stephen Leinen, *Gay Cops,* New Brunswick, N.J.: Rutgers University Press, 1993.
10. *New York Times,* November 10, 1993.
11. "Court: Shareholders Can Challenge Cracker Barrel's Anti-gay Policies," United Press International, October 19, 1993.

"A new culture has sprung up . . . a pioneering group of teenagers who identify themselves as gay or lesbian. They challenge a hundred years of social oppression, secrecy, and silence on the rights of those who desire the same sex, when they "come out of the closet" and courageously reveal themselves to their families, friends, teachers and employers. . . . These youth are a new cultural phenomenon: a generation who identify as lesbian or gay, the first ever in human history."

Gilbert Herdt and Andrew Boxer,
Children of Horizons, 1993

Documentation has only recently become available to support what many in the lesbian and gay community have long suspected: gay and lesbian youth are extremely isolated and at exceptionally high risk for suicide, drug use, homelessness, and HIV. At the same time, however, growing numbers of young people are choosing to "come out" within the context of high schools and colleges. The impact that these youth have on the educational system has yet to be documented. For example, precisely how many lesbian and gay youth—and, for that matter, lesbian and gay teachers—are visible within high schools, and how does this visibility affect attitudes and perceptions of students and teachers?

YOUTH

As many as 7.2 million Americans under age 20 are lesbian or gay. [1]

According to Kinsey, 28% of boys and 17% of girls have one or more same-sex experiences before age 20. [2]

In a 1992 study of lesbian and gay youths in Chicago, the mean age for the first same-sex sexual experience was 15.2 for females and 13.1 for males. [3]

In the same study, 64% of the males and 50% of the females said their self-esteem was affected positively by "coming out." [3]

The average age at which lesbians "come out" is between 16 and 19; the average age at which gay males "come out" is between 14 and 16. [2]

Half of all lesbian and gay youths interviewed in a 1987 study report that their parents rejected them for being gay. [2]

1 in 4 gay and lesbian youths are forced to leave home on account of conflicts with their families about being gay. [2]

Gay and lesbian youths constitute up to 25% of all youths living on the streets in the United States. [4]

Up to half of the gay and bisexual males forced out of their homes engage in prostitution to support themselves. [2]

80% of lesbian and gay youths who took part in a 1987 study reported severe isolation. [2]

In a 1988 survey of males ages 15 to 19, 89% said they found the idea of sex between two men "disgusting." Only 12% felt confident that they could befriend a gay person. [5]

Every day, 13 Americans ages 15 to 24 commit suicide. In 1989, suicide was the leading cause of death among gay, lesbian, bisexual, and transgendered youths. [4]

Lesbian and gay youths are 2 to 3 times more likely to attempt suicide than their heterosexual peers. Gay and lesbian youths account for up to 30% of all completed suicides among youths. [4]

In a 1991 study of 137 gay and bisexual male youths, 30% had attempted suicide once and 13% reported multiple attempts. The mean age of those attempting suicide was 15.5. Three quarters of first attempts came after the youth had labeled himself a homosexual. [6]

53% of transsexual youths surveyed in 1981 had attempted suicide. [4]

The Spring 1993 edition of the Hetrick-Martin Institute's *You Are Not Alone: National Lesbian, Gay and Bisexual Youth Organization Directory* lists more than 170 support groups, hotlines, and other agencies and organizations that provide counseling, emergency shelter, medical care, and other services to gay, lesbian, and bisexual youth. [7]

EDUCATION

52% of Americans surveyed in 1993 opposed teaching about gay orientation in sex-education classes in public schools. [8]

Since 1982, more than 1,600 school districts have adopted sex-education curricula that present sexual abstinence and monogamy within heterosexual marriage as the only sexual choices available to teenagers. [9]

There are approximately 3,600,000 teachers employed in the United States. Using Kinsey's findings, there are an estimated 360,000 lesbian and gay teachers—a number equal to more than the entire teaching staffs of California and Minnesota. [10]

In a 1990 study, 74 gay and lesbian teachers and 66 heterosexual teachers took a psychological test that predicts success in the classroom: there was no difference between the two groups' scores. [11]

In a 1987 study conducted by the South Carolina Guidance Counselors' Association, 8 of 10 prospective teachers and nearly two-thirds of guidance counselors expressed negative feelings about homosexuality and about lesbians and gay men. [10]

Citizens for Excellence in Education, a right-wing group based in Costa Mesa, California, says that more than 2,000 of its members have been elected to school boards across the United States. [9]

45% of gay males and 20% of lesbians experience physical or verbal assault in high school. 28% of these young people feel forced to drop out of school due to harassment based on sexual orientation. [2]

In a 1989 study of gay male youths, 69% reported a history of school problems related to sexual identity. [12]

In 1988, there were no gay/straight student alliances in private high schools. As of 1993, at least 16 independent schools had such alliances, while 17 had at least one openly gay teacher. [13]

The number of public schools in Massachusetts with a gay/straight alliance rose from 2 in 1992 to 20 in 1993. [14]

Nationally, there were more than 100 lesbian and gay support groups in high schools as of 1993. [14]

In December 1993, Massachusetts became the first and only state in the country to outlaw discrimination against lesbian and gay students in public schools. [15]

Oberlin Gay Liberation, founded in 1971, was the first lesbian, gay, and bisexual student organization in the United States. [16]

As of January 1992, 15 U.S. colleges and universities had lesbian, gay, and bisexual task forces or offices. At least 43 offer some sort of lesbian, gay, or bisexual courses, and 248 have nondiscrimination policies that include sexual orientation. [17]

In surveys from 1985 to 1989 at Yale University, Rutgers University, Pennsylvania State University, the University of Massachusetts at Amherst, and the University of Illinois, between 45% and 76% of gay and lesbian students said they were verbally threatened or harassed. An average of 90% of these incidents went unreported. [10]

In a survey of the general student body of Oberlin College, 78%–88% of students had overheard stereotypical or derogatory remarks about lesbians and gay men; 93%–96% supported the presence of lesbians and gay men on campus, but 9%–25% said they felt the need to conceal their support. [10]

As of the spring of 1993, 40% of the African American male tenured faculty at Harvard College was gay. [18]

As of the spring of 1993, there were 5 African American male professors among the tenured faculty at Harvard College. [18]

SOURCES

1. *Statistical Abstract of the United States,* Washington, D.C.: U.S. Bureau of the Census, 1992; and Kinsey's estimates.
2. "Factfile: Lesbian, Gay, and Bisexual Youth," Hetrick-Martin Institute, 1992.
3. Gilbert Herdt and Andrew Boxer, *Children of Horizons,* Boston: Beacon, 1993.
4. U.S. Department of Health and Human Services, "Report of the Secretary's Task Force on Youth Suicide," 1989.

5. William Marsiglio, "Attitudes toward Homosexual Activity and Gays as Friends: A National Survey of Heterosexual 15-to-19-Year-Old Males," *Journal of Sex Research* 30, February 1993.

6. Gary Remafedi, James A. Farrow, and Robert W. Deisher, "Risk Factors for Attempted Suicide in Gay and Bisexual Youth," *Pediatrics* 87, June 1991.

7. Hetrick-Martin Institute, *You Are Not Alone: National Lesbian, Gay, and Bisexual Youth Organization Directory,* Spring 1993.

8. Joseph P. Shapiro et al., "Straight Talk about Gays," *U.S. News & World Report,* July 5, 1993.

9. Chris Bull, "Why Johnny Can't Learn about Condoms: How the Religious Right Censors Sex Education across the U.S.," *The Advocate,* December 15, 1992.

10. Karen M. Harbeck, ed., *Coming Out of the Classroom Closet: Gay and Lesbian Students, Teachers and Curricula,* Binghamton, N.Y.: Harrington Park, 1992.

11. M. Martin, "Gay, Lesbian, and Heterosexual Teachers: Acceptance of Self, Acceptance of Others." Unpublished report, 1990.

12. Gary Remafedi, "Adolescent Homosexuality," *Pediatrics* 79, March 1987.

13. *Speaking Out: A Forum for Sexual Minority Issues in the Boarding School Community* 2, November 1993.

14. Mike Dorning, "Schools' Support Groups Helping Gay Teens to Cope," *Chicago Tribune,* November 30, 1993.

15. Sara Rimer, "Rights for Gay Students in Public Schools," *New York Times,* December 12, 1993.

16. Lynne Yamaguchi Fletcher, *The First Gay Pope and Other Records,* Boston: Alyson, 1992.

17. National Gay and Lesbian Task Force, Washington, D.C., 1993.

18. "Passion and Pain Mark Speeches at Anti-Powell Rally," *Harvard Gay & Lesbian Newsletter* 11, Spring 1993.